THE INFANT FORMULA FEEDING CONTROVERSY

AN ANNOTATED BIBLIOGRAPHY
1970-1984

John A. Sparks, J.D., *Editor*
Victor E. Vouga, J.D. and
L. John Van Til, Ph.D., *Contributing Editors*

Kendall/Hunt
Publishing Company
Dubuque, Iowa

Public Policy Education Fund Inc.
161 E. Pine Street
Grove City, PA 16127

Printed in the United States of America   **B**   403739   01

TABLE OF CONTENTS

PREFACE AND ACKNOWLEDGEMENTS

In the early 1970s the first rumblings were heard of what would soon become a full-fledged public debate about the formula feeding of infants in the less-developed world. Because a Swiss firm, Nestle S.A., was one of the largest producers and marketers of infant formula in developing countries, it became the target of a boycott, by critic groups, of its consumer products. Nestle was not the only infant food manufacturer criticized, however, more attention was drawn to Nestle than to other producers.

As is true with many issues of the day, popular interest first rose and then waned. However, the enduring meanings of all the exchanges, charges, counter-charges, resolutions, and boycotts remain to be studied in the quieter waters of reflection.

Public Policy Education Fund, Inc. has compiled and annotated this bibliography of the infant formula feeding controversy in order to aid those who have the task of interpreting the set of events involving various infant formula manufacturers and various church and critic groups during much of the 1970s and early 1980s.

We are grateful to The Nestle Coordination Center for Nutrition for opening its extensive periodicals and newspaper files to us on the infant formula controversy. We are appreciative of the cooperation shown by Interfaith Center on Corporate Responsibility and by the Infant Formula Action Coalition in furnishing us with documents and materials about their campaign and viewpoint. In addition, we are grateful to the staff members of the Grove City College Library, Grove City, Pennsylvania, Diane Grundy, Librarian, and to the University of Pittsburgh Library for the help that they provided in locating and copying documents.

I thank my wife, Marion Sparks, for the careful review and proofing of the annotations and for her persistent effort to help us meet the many deadlines which are required for the production of such a bibliography. We deeply appreciate the long hours spent by our able secretary, Mrs. Ellie Kendall, in entering into the computer the bibliographic data.

Finally, we are indebted to the many supporters and friends of Public Policy Education Fund, Inc. for their encouragement.

John A. Sparks
President
Public Policy Education Fund, Inc.

THE ANNOTATED BIBLIOGRAPHY — ITS ORGANIZATION AND USE

The bibliography's basic categories illustrate the fact that modern public debates grow to have an almost "human-like" quality to them. Public issues seem to have a birth, a period of maturity and then a demise. The length of the "life-cycle" of a controversial question is affected by mass media exposure, the intensity created by visual images, and the appeal that the issue can make to a variety of existing action groups as well as groups created to address the issue.

The formula feeding controversy lasted over a period running from 1970 to 1984 although interest in the popular boycott accelerated and reached a peak from 1977 to 1981. The headings of the five main sections, therefore, are chronological, which is to say that each main heading covers a period of years which roughly marks the beginning, maturing and the winding down of the dispute. They are set out here:

I.   The Birth of the Controversy 1970-73

II. Public Awareness, The Popular Campaign, and the Industry Response 1974-77

III. The Boycott Phase — Expansion of the Popular Campaign 1978-81

IV. The Phase of the WHO Code and the Industry Response 1982-83

V.   The End of the Controversy 1984

Within each major heading are six (A-F) subheadings listed below, with each subheading covering the **type** of material annotated. A subheading will be used **only** where there are materials which fit that category. Each individual annotation is numbered and all references in the index are to the numbers of the annotations. Organization within subheadings is alphabetical by author or source of publication if unsigned. The six subheadings are:

A. General Articles and Studies

B. Scientific Articles and Studies

C. News Articles

D. Critic Groups

E. Church Publications

F. Infant Food Industry Publications

Certain materials seemed to defy simple classification, however, the rationale for subheadings (A-F) is set out here to aid the researcher.

A. General Articles and Studies — Included under this classification are those articles, studies, and books in which the author covers the **whole** of the issues of the controversy, that is, articles which are comprehensive rather than narrowly focused. Included, too, would be those items which cover the **general background** for understanding the formula dispute.

B. Scientific Articles and Studies — Included under this category are technical and scientific articles. The subject matter of these items will usually be **narrower** than in category "A". Usually medical or scientific questions are concentrated upon. Concomitantly, the questions considered will normally be taken up in greater depth. Studies often fall into this category where there are strict geographic limits on the conclusions, for example, the breastfeeding activities of a small African village. In classifying the item as scientific, the annotator first looked to the subject and the way in which it was treated, then to the type of journal in which it was published, and, finally, to the authorship.

C. News Articles — The articles under this category are often informational, that is, they chronicle the major developments in the controversy. They usually contain less analysis than the other categories. The sources are generally newspapers, but that is not entirely true since magazines and other journals contain news sections. Most often news items do not contain bibliographic references, nor are the references made in the articles to other sources footnoted. Editorials are included here as well. Since the volume of news items is so great, the inclusion of articles or items in this section must be highly selective.

D. Critic Groups — Various groups — some existing, some newly formed — popularized the causes which surrounded the controversy. Their materials are included under this classification. The appellation "critic" is chosen as a more neutral term than others which have been used. Basically, these groups and organizations counseled certain **action.** They were not primarily concerned with dispassionate analysis. They were openly engaged in advocacy of a particular stance on the issues raised.

E. Church Publications — Various denominational groups and lesser divisions and regions within the major denominations considered the issues of the formula feeding controversy. Some issued resolutions at one point in the controversy and withdrew them later. The materials generated by the religious community are included under this category. Often these materials were more difficult to obtain than others because they were circulated to church members for their consideration.

F. Infant Food Industry Publications — During the controversy various infant food manufacturers published papers, distributed materials, and issued news releases. In addition, certain manufacturers, including Nestle, formed the International Council of Infant Food Industries (ICIFI) to coordinate industry efforts to oversee industry marketing standards for infant foods. The publications of the manufacturers and of ICIFI are included in this section.

Late in the controversy Nestle created an audit commission chaired by former Senator Edmund Muskie. The commission reviewed complaints of marketing violations and issued a number of quarterly reports. These reports are also annotated in this section.

Indexes — Two indexes, one to authors' names and one to publications, are available at the back of the volume. Citations in the indexes refer to annotation numbers, **not** to page numbers.

Final Note

Publication deadlines meant that in a few cases materials were not received in time to be included.

THE INFANT FORMULA CONTROVERSY — AN OVERVIEW

I. The Major Issues and the Researcher

The mass of writing and speaking done about the formula feeding controversy raised a list of important, yet complex, questions. The questions are difficult because they have scientific, ethical, economic and emotional dimensions to them and because they involve the difficult task of verification — that is, telling whether something is true or false, probable or improbable. Jacque Barzon and Henry F. Graff point out (The Modern Researcher, Revised ed. New York: Harcourt, Brace & World, Inc., 1970) that *verification is a combination of attention to detail, common-sense, reasoning, familiarity with human behavior, solid judgment, disentangling facts from ideology and understanding causation.* If all of the above are done well, the writing or speaking produced will faithfully reveal reality. If the above elements are ignored, then what is produced will be a distortion of reality. What then are the principal questions raised by the Nestle controversy?

II. The Principal Issues

For the early infancy of Third World children there is virtually no disagreement that breast milk is the optimal food.[1] Of course, it is understood that other provisions must be made for the feeding of infants whose mothers are sick or deceased.[2] However, even in early infancy some writers observe that the use of formula is quite common among working mothers, urbanized mothers or mothers who fail to produce sufficient milk.[3]

A. What Explains Feeding Choice?

The first major question argued from various perspectives during the controversy was: What explains the choice made by mothers for formula feeding as opposed to breastfeeding?

Some observers say that mothers choose formula primarily because of the promotional activities of infant formula companies either directly to consumers or indirectly through health professionals and hospitals.[4] Others observe that government programs of free formula distribution[5] play an important part in encouraging formula use. Still other writers emphasize the impact of urban culture and the need to work on the breastfeeding versus the artificial feeding decision of mothers.[6] Moreover, other explanations such as income level and family size are seen as the most important determinants of the breast/artificial feeding choice.[7].

B. The Supplementation Issue

Another area of dispute is the proper point in the infant's development at which artificial feeding ought to begin. Some scientists contend that beyond three or four months there is a danger that if breastfeeding continues to be the **sole source** of nutrition for the infant, the infant's rate of growth will be slowed because protein and energy demands will outrun the nutrients of mother's milk alone.[8] Mixed feeding, that is breastfeeding supplemented by some kind of artificial feeding, is found to be the most common mode of feeding in less-developed countries according to many studies.[9]

Another widely cited study refers to mixed feeding and sets six months as the time after which supplementation of mother's milk is necessary in less-developed countries.[10] Some authors take the position that the lower quantity of milk production in malnourished Third World mothers, coupled with the low birth weight of their children, make early supplementation with a nutritious feed extremely important.[11] Although it was little talked about during the controversy, the need for some kind of supplementation after early infancy is well-established by the scientific literature.

C. The Dangers of Disease

Yet another issue could be stated this way: Is the use of commercial formula or the use of native gruels as supplements dangerous to the health of Third World infants?

Commercial formula is **not** inherently dangerous. As properly manufactured it does not contain harmful bacteria, for instance, which would present a threat to infants. The position of infant food industry opponents is that Third World mothers often do not properly prepare the commercial formula, because they fail to boil water and they over-dilute the formula.[12] On the other hand, one author concludes that over-dilution did occur but that boiling of water was done in over 90% of the preparations.[13] The one problem with the argument of "unsanitary preparation" which was raised during the controversy against formula purveyors, is that such an argument applies equally well to native weaning or supplemental foods as scientists have pointed out, especially if one adds that weaning foods are often kept for days at ambient temperatures.[14] In addition, environmental contamination from sources other than the feeding bottle may carry disease to the growing infant.[15]

D. Breastfeeding and Health

Some studies make a positive correlation between the relative health of the child and breastfeeding, while drawing negative conclusions about health and bottle feeding.[16] To begin with, "bottle feeding" is an ambiguous term since it may mean: formula feeding exclusively, formula feeding as supplementation, the feeding of starchy native weaning foods exclusively, or the mixed feeding of native foods, formula, and breastfeeding. The studies which make comparisons between artificial feeding and breastfeeding are often flawed by methodological defects including mistakes in sampling, errors of confounding differences in the sample, and faulty reasoning from the evidence.[17]

The complex reality is that breastfeeding after four to six months must be supplemented by other feeding. These supplements, commercial or native, are necessary but create some additional exposure of the children to disease due to poor preparation and generally unsanitary conditions. However, the scientific evidence is flawed when it comes to asserting a general correlation between breast and artificial feeding and health or morbidity.

E. Is Breastfeeding on the Decline in the Developing World?

Breastfeeding is on the decline in the Third World say some observers.[18] Others, including the World Health Organization, see a strong traditional and deeply rooted attachment to breastfeeding in the developing world.[19]

III. Other Principal Issues

A. Industry Self-Regulation and Responsiveness

During the controversy a great deal of argument occurred about whether the infant food industry could regulate itself and effectively respond to its critics.[20] There is evidence that industry members did respond in various constructive ways. Certain observers saw the industry positions as unresponsive and generally uncooperative,[21] and others as a combination of these.[22]

B. The Question of Credibility

The issue of the credibility of the Nestle response to the WHO Code (adopted May 1981) became **the** central issue of the **latter** part of the controversy. Whether or not Nestle S.A. was continuing to promote formula in ways that were in violation of the Code became the main concern of boycotters. Predictably, some groups and writers complained of non-compliance.[23] Others were more patient and commendatory.[24]

C. The Issue of the Audit Commission

Since the question of Nestle compliance with the WHO Code was the only remaining issue on which real controversy was still thriving and because Nestle itself could not seem to satisfy opposing critic groups that its efforts to curtail direct advertising and to otherwise comply with the Code were effective, the Nestle Infant Formula Audit Commission was formed.[25] It was composed of independent members with a budget which the Commission controlled although the funds were from Nestle. The Commission insisted upon documented, high-quality evidence from Nestle and from those who charged Nestle with Code violations. That insistence, Nestle's ability to overcome the natural lags of implementing policies, and its willingness to make reasonable changes, led to the eventual suspension of the boycott,[26] and finally, to its termination.[27]

Though the public controversy is ended, the sorting out of the deeper meanings of the questions raised still remains to be done.

John A. Sparks, J.D.
President
Public Policy Education Fund, Inc.
1985 Grove City, PA

---

[1]Protein Advisory Group of the United Nations System, statement No. 23, July 18, 1972.

[2]John A. Sparks, "The Nestle Controversy — Another Look", (Grove City, PA. Public Policy Education Fund, Inc.) 1982.

[3]Adeoye Adeniyi, "The Place of Artificial Feeding in Africa" Statement, IDR(I)-26-GB; C. Itenran, "Nutritional Evaluation of Breastfeeding Practices in the Far East". *Environmental Child Health* pp. 63-7 April 1976; Alan Berg. "The Economics of Breastfeeding" *Saturday Review of Science* April 28, 1973; Sara Nerlove, "Women's Workload and Infant Feeding Practices: A Relationship with Demographic Implications" *Ethnology* Vol. 13(2): 207-214, 1974.

[4]D. B. Jelliffe, "Commerciogenic Malnutrition" *Nutrition Review* 30: 199-205 September, 1972; T. Greiner, "The Promotion of Bottle Feeding by Multinational Corporations . . ." *Cornell International Monograph* No. 2, Cornell University, 1975; Mike Muller, "The Baby Killer" London: War on Want, May 1974; D. B. Jelliffe and E. F. P. Jelliffe, "Breast Is Best: Modern Meanings" *New England Journal of Medicine* 297: 912-5 October 27, 1977; D. B. Jelliffe and E. F. P. Jelliffe, "Feeding Young Infants in Developing Countries: Comments on the Future Situation and Future Needs", *Studies in Family Planning* 9(8): 227-29, August 1978; James E. Post, "Testimony Before the U.S. Subcommittee on Health and Scientific Research of the Committee on Human Resources, May 23, 1978.

[5]"A Swedish Code of Ethics of Infant Foods", Scandanavian Pediatrics Association, *Acta Paed Scand* 66: 129-32, 1977.

[6]Dana Raphael, "The Politics of Breastfeeding" *American Academy of Pediatrics,* December 1981, pp. 14-15; J. D. Gussler. and L. H. Breesemeister, "The Insufficient Milk Syndrome: A Biocultural Explanation, *Medical Anthropology* 4: 3-24, 1980.

[7]A. E. Dugdale, "Breastfeeding in a South East Asia City", *Far East Medical Journal* 6:230-4, 1970.

[8]A. M. Thomson and A. E. Black, "Nutritional Aspects of Human Lactation" *World Health Organization Bulletin,* 52:163, 1975; R. G. Whitehead and M. G. M. Rowland, "A Brief Account of . . . Nutrition . . . in the Gambia from 1974 to November 1975" (unpublished draft).

[9]S. Orwell and J. Murray, "Infant Feeding and Health in Ibadan", *Environmental Child Health* August 1974, pp. 206-19; *Infant Feeding in the Developing Countries,* Nestle Products Technical Assistance Co. Ltd. Switzerland, 1977; J. Mauron and H. R. Muller, "The Problem of Malnutrition", and "Nutrition and Infant Mortality:, Nestle S.A., 1976; Lee Edson, "Babies In Poverty: The Real Victims of the Breast/Bottle Controversy" *The Lactation Review* Vol. IV, No. 1, 1979, pp. 21-38; Mary M. Kent, "Breastfeeding in the Developing World: Current Patterns and Implications for Future Trends: *World Fertility Survey,* Population Reference Bureau, Inc., 1981.

[10]"The Rural Kenyan Nutrition Survey, Feb.-March, 1977" *Social Perspectives,* Central Bureau of Statistics, Ministry of Finance and Planning, Government of Kenya, Sept. 1977; W. Tarnow-Mordi, "Infant Malnutrition in Africa: The Role of Artificial Milk Feeds", *Environmental Child Health* October 1974, pp. 239-41.

[11]Jose Villar and J. M. Belizan, "Breastfeeding in Developing Countries", *The Lancet,* September 19, 1981, p. 623; George M. Guthrie, "WHO Infant Formula Code Misses Real Problem", *Sharon Herald,* May 30, 1981; R. G. Whitehead, et. al. "Factors Influencing Lactation Performance in Rural Gambian Mothers", *The Lancet,* July 22, 1978 pp. 178-81; R. G. Whitehead and A. A. Paul, "Infant Growth and Human Milk Requirements", *The Lancet,* July 25, 1981.

[12]Margulies, Leah, "Marketing and Promotion of Infant Formula and the Decline of Breastfeeding in Underdeveloped Countries", Testimony before U.S. Subcommittee on Health and Scientific Research of the Committee on Human Resources, May 23, 1978; D. Surgono, et. al. "Bacterial Contamination and Dilution of Milk in Infant Feeding Bottles", *Journal of Tropical Pediatrics* April, 1980.

[13]S. K. Reddy, "Artificial Feeding in Jamaica and Barbados", *West Indian Medical Journal* Vol. XX:207, 1971.
[14]A. A. O. Laditan and P. J. Reeds, "A Study of the Age of Onset, Diet and Importance of Infection...in Nigeria," *British Journal of Nutrition* 36:411-19, 1976; M. G. M. Rowland et. al. "The Weanlings Dilemma, Bacterial Contamination in Traditional Gambian Weaning Foods", *The Lancet,* January 21, 1976, p. 236; M. G. M. Rowland and R. A. E. Barrell, "Infant Foods as a Potential Source of Diarrhoeal Illness in Rural West Africa", *Transactions of the Royal Society of Tropical Medicine and Hygiene,* Vol. 73, No. 1, 1979, p. 85.
[15]Fernando Monckeberg, "Crying Over Spilled Milk: *Creces,* 1981, pp. 25-7.
[16]James Finebrace, "Imported Milk Powders and Bottle Feeding: The Evidence from the Yemen Arab Republic" (1979, London); D. B. Jelliffe, "Feeding Young Infants in Developing Countries", *Journal of Tropical Pediatrics and Environmental Child Health* 24(4):155-7 August 1978; Spencer A. Larsen and Daryl R. Homer, "Relation of Breast versus Bottle Feeding to Hospitalization for Gastroenteritis in Middle Class U.S. Population, *The Journal of Pediatrics* 92(32):417-18, March 1978.
[17]H. S. Sauls, "Potential Effect of Demographic and Other Variables in Studies Comparing Morbidity of Breastfed and Bottlefed Babies", *Pediatrics* 64:523-7, October 1979; E. Cole "Breastfeeding: A Critique of the Literature" in D. Raphael Breastfeeding and Food Policy in a Hungry World, New York: Academic Press, 1979; Fred D. Miller, Jr., *Out of the Mouths of Babes: The Infant Formula Controversy,* Bowling Green State University, 1983.
[18]Michael B. Bader, "Breast Feeding: The Role of Multinational Corporations in Latin America", *International Journal of Health Science* 6(4):609-26, 1976; Mike Muller, "Money, Milk, Marasmus" *New Scientist,* February 18, 1974; N. Baumslaug and E. Sabin, "Perspectives in Maternal-Infant Nutrition" *HEW* Office of International Health, Sept. 1978; J. Knodel and N. Debavalya, "Breast-Feeding Trends in Thailand and Their Demographic Impact", *Intercom,* March 1981, pp. 8-10.
[19]C. Itenran, op. cit. J. Knodel and N. Dabavalya (Knodel is cited here again because he concludes that though there has been a decline in the duration of breastfeeding, it is still relatively long — 17.5 months in rural areas and 8.4 months in urban areas.) M. Popkin, et. al. "Breast-Feeding Practices in Low Income Countries, Patterns and Determinants", *Carolina Population Center Papers* No. 11, October 1979 and B. M. Popkin, "Breast-Feeding Patterns in Low-Income Countries" *Science* 218:1088-93, December 10, 1982.
[20]"Code of Ethics and Professional Standards for Advertising, Product Information and Advisory Services for Breast-Milk Substitutes" ICIFI (International Council of Infant Food Industries) 1977; ICIFI: A Review of Its Objectives and Activities" Pamphlet, September 1977; Edwin M. Epstein and Lee E. Preston, eds. "The Infant Formula Issue: A Case Study" in *Business Environment/Public Policy: The Field and Its Future* (Proceedings of the Am. Assoc. of Collegiate Schools of Business Summer Conference, St. Louis, Mo., 1981); Henry G. Ciocca, "The Nestle Boycott as a Corporate Learning Experience", the Nestle Company, Inc., March 18, 1980.
[21]Edward Baer and Leah Margulies, "Infant and Young Child Feeding: An Analysis of the WHO/UNICEF Meeting", *Studies in Family Planning* 11(2):72-75, February 1980. See also numerous publications of INFACT and Interfaith Center on Corporate Responsibility cited in the bibliography.
[22]Thorton Bradshaw and David Vogel, *Corporations and Their Critics: Issues and Answers to the Problems of Corporate Social Responsibility* New York: McGraw-Hill Book Company, 1981; James E. Post, Corporate Behavior and Social Change Reston, Va.: Reston Publishing Co., Inc. 1978.
[23]"Infant Formula Promotion, 1981". A Report by the International Baby Food Action Network (IBFAN), May 1981; "Breaking the Rules" IBFAN, May 1982; "Confronting the U.S. Infant Formula Giants" *Corporate Examiner* July/August 1982 Vol. II, No. 7-8; Leah Margulies, "Ten Points of Clarification on the Nestle Boycott", New York: ICCR, July 1983.
[24]Roy Howard Beck, "Formula Debate Takes a New Turn", *United Methodist Reporter* February 4, 1983; "Nestle Boycott Mediation Efforts, and Christian Ethical Teaching", *United Methodist Reporter* October 30, 1981.
[25]Charter, The Nestle Infant Formula Audit Commission (NIFAC), Nestle Coordination Center for Nutrition, Inc., Washington, D.C., May 1982.
[26]Edmund S. Muskie, *Nestle Infant Formula Audit Commission: First Quarterly Report,* September 30, 1982; NIFAC: *Second Quarterly Report,* Dec. 31, 1981; NIFAC: *Third Quarterly Report,* June 30, 1983; *Transcript of Proceedings* Washington, D.C., January 26, 1984.
[27]"Joint Statement of Nestle and The International Nestle Boycott Committee, October 4, 1984." Washington, D.C.: Nestle Coordination Center for Nutrition, Inc., October 4, 1984.

I. THE BIRTH OF THE CONTROVERSY: 1970-1973

A. GENERAL ARTICLES AND STUDIES

001. Aykroyd, W. R.
"Protein-Calorie Malnutrition." In: <u>Conquest of Deficiency Diseases</u>. WHO
Basic Study 24:50, 1970.

This chapter is an excellent introduction to protein-calorie malnutrition
and the various forms it takes — marasmus and kwashiorkor. The
author first defines protein-calorie malnutrition and then describes
various factors which lead to its existence. The use of unhygienic
feeding methods at weaning and from then on subjects the child to
infectious bacteria and eventually to gastroenteritis. The prevalence
of protein-calorie malnutrition has not been measured by statistically
acceptable methods in most of the less-developed countries. Infant
mortality rates are the best single indicator of community health
including, of course, infant health. The post-neonatal death rates in
developing countries are reducible by public health means and improved nutritional information and practices. Urbanization, because
it often leads to earlier weaning, helps to promote protein-calorie
malnutrition, but urbanization also helps to combat protein-calorie
malnutrition because urban dwellers are better educated and receive
higher quality health services.

002. Aykroyd, W. R.
"Nutrition and Mortality in Infancy and Early Childhood: Past and Present
Relationships." *American Journal of Clinical Nutrition* 24:480, 1971.

The author deals with the rates of infant mortality in England in 1906
and explains the most frequent causes of death as then recorded. They
were described as: "diarrhoea and enteritis" and "atrophy and debili-
ty". One important health commentator thought that faulty artificial
feeding was the most important cause of infant mortality. Protein-calorie malnutrition in the less-developed world can perhaps be overcome
by the same means which tended to eliminate similar malnutrition in
England many decades ago, namely, increased health services and
the creation and promotion of the hygienic use of inexpensive artificial
feeds.

003. Beaver, M. W.
"Population, Infant Mortality and Milk." *Population Studies* 27:243, 1973.

The author suggests the decline in infant mortality rates in England
and Wales from 1840 to 1900 and beyond coincides with new developments in the dairy industry such as pasteurization and, later, widely
available dried milk used in infant feeding. Commercial innovations
were beneficial, not detrimental, in helping to decrease infant mortality.

004. Berg, Alan.
"Crisis in Infant Feeding Practices." In: <u>The Nutrition Factor</u>. The Brookings
Institution, 1973.

Nutrition planner, Berg, argues that where breastfeeding has declined
and has been replaced by the use of cow's milk, an economic burden

has been placed on those who have made such a choice in that breast milk would have been relatively less expensive to produce than milk from animal sources. Berg cites certain studies in South America and Asia which show a decline in breastfeeding. He emphasizes the urban mother's shift to breast milk substitutes. Interestingly, Berg does not condemn infant formula companies alone for the decline of breastfeeding. He discusses how the Chilean government's distribution of free powdered milk is an example of how governments can do harm to traditional patterns of breastfeeding even though they are trying to help their own people. Note that Berg cites the Swiss policy of subsidizing mothers who will breastfeed a certain length of time, a policy begun in 1911.

005. Brown, Roy E.
"Breast Feeding in Modern Times." *American Journal of Clinical Nutrition* 26:556, 1973.

This article is a strong plea for breastfeeding instead of bottle feeding. The author attributes some of the changing outlook toward breastfeeding to urbanization, but he is also convinced that the active promotion of infant formula has had a great deal to do with the trend. The author also states that the responsibility for promoting breastfeeding rests with health professionals. This very early article contains all the statements about formula feeding, more accurately, bottle feeding, which are found in later articles by the opponents of formula feeding.

006. Hendrickse, R. G. and David Morley.
"The Baby Food Tragedy." *New Internationalist* 6:8, August 1973.

Tropical medicine experts Hendrickse and Morley say that, in part, the marketing of infant formula in developing countries by Western corporations has contributed to the problem of infants suffering from diarrheal disease and gastroenteritis. Factors other than advertising have been responsible for the trend away from breastfeeding where it has occurred.

007. Jelliffe, D. B.
"Commerciogenic Malnutrition? Time For a Dialogue." *Food Technology* 25:55, February 1971.

In this and a similarly titled article published a year and a half later, Jelliffe states that commercial enterprises with excellent worldwide reputations have exported various infant foods to less-developed countries possibly resulting in more harm than good because of the great differences of economic levels, hygiene, and maternal education. Among his examples are what he terms "highly expensive infant milk preparations". He calls the malnutrition which results "commerciogenic malnutrition". Subsequent writers often refer to this article.

008. Jelliffe, D. B.
"Commerciogenic Malnutrition." *Nutrition Review* 30:199, September 1972.
Jelliffe claims a real need to re-examine Western nutrition influences in less-developed countries. He does see hope in the activities of the

U.N. Protein Advisory Group, and calls upon firms, health workers, government policy-makers, and others to reassess this whole area of infant feeding.

009. Orr, Elizabeth.
"The Use of Protein-Rich Foods for the Relief of Malnutrition in Developing Countries: An Analysis of Experience." *Tropical Products Institute Report G73,* August 1972.

Part of the general setting out of which the formula feeding controversy has arisen has been the need for high quality weaning foods. This monograph deals with the nutritional make-up and the cost of such protein-rich foods and their distribution and acceptance among various low income groups. The relatively high cost of these supplements and the many problems of distributing to more remote areas make their use to combat malnutrition very difficult.

010. Popkin, B. M. and M. C. Latham.
"The Limitations and Dangers of Commerciogenic Nutritious Foods." *American Journal of Clinical Nutrition* 26:1015, 1973.

The contributors to this article state a simple, often repeated theme: commercial food products developed in the West are often improperly marketed in Third World countries with the help of AID dollars and advice. This article is important to the formula feeding controversy because it sets that dispute in the larger context of opposition to Western products in the less-developed world. The authors want controls on advertising, free food for the needy, and subsidized food for the poor. They also advocate the development of indigenous foods, a point on which development economists would have some disagreement.

011. Raphael, Dana.
"When Mothers Need Mothering." *New York Times Magazine* February 8, 1970.

This is a thoughtful essay on the virtues of breastfeeding and its effects on the mother. It also exhorts experienced mothers to provide special care and training for new mothers.

012. Sadre, M., E. Emawis and G. Donoso.
"The Changing Pattern of Malnutrition." *Ecology of Food and Nutrition* 1:55, 1971.

The authors believe that malnutrition among children will change from later life (second and third year) kwashiorkor to earlier occurring marasmus. The writers suggest that early weaning to bottle fed cow's milk diets, feeding of low nutritional foods and preparation of infant foods in unhygienic conditions lead to marasmus. Breastfeeding is discouraged by the uncertainties of urban living and the advertising of commercial baby foods.

013. Willot, Norris.
"How Nestle Adapts Its Products to Its Markets." *Business Abroad* p. 32, June 1970.

The sale of products into different countries and cultures depends upon being able to adapt to differences in local tastes and customs. That is the message of this short article about international marketing which takes Nestle as its example. The piece was obviously written before the formula feeding controversy but it gives the reader an idea of how one food company saw itself and how others saw it at that earlier time.

B. SCIENTIFIC ARTICLES AND STUDIES

014. Berg, Alan.
"The Economics of Breastfeeding." *Saturday Review of the Sciences* April 28, 1973.

Berg regards the decline of breastfeeding in urban cultures of the Third World as placing a real economic burden on these already poor countries. His assessment of the blame for such a decline as derived from the examples which he presents is a combination of urbanization and government programs which often urge the use of dried milk or other artificial feeds.

015. Cantrelle, P., and H. Leridon.
"Breastfeeding, Mortality in Childhood and Fertility in a Rural Zone of Senegal." *Population Studies* 25:505, 1971.

Longer periods of breastfeeding lengthened the interval between births in Niakhar, Senegal, according to the findings of the study. No contraceptive practices were known. The mere practice of continuing breastfeeding, however, did not prevent conception while the previous child was still being nursed. New conception occurred in about one third of the cases where breastfeeding continued.

016. Dugdale, A. E.
"Breastfeeding in a South East Asia City." *Far East Medical Journal* 6:230, 1970.

This study took place in Kuala Lumpur, the capital of Malaysia. Infant feeding practices of urban mothers were studied, and in almost all groups, mothers with high family incomes breastfed less than those with low family incomes. For Chinese and Indian mothers, family size did not seem to be important to breastfeeding decisions, but among Malay mothers, breastfeeding was more common among families with two to four children. For the period studied, some groups increased their incidence of breastfeeding while others decreased.

017. Graham, George C.
"Environmental Factors Affecting the Growth of Children." *American Journal of Clinical Nutrition* 25:1184, 1972.

The author discusses an ongoing study of various factors which affect the growth of malnourished children studied prospectively in Lima, Peru. Among many interesting observations the author notes that even severely malnourished infants can make catch-up growth progress if they are put in a healthy environment where they receive adequate nutrients. Marital status of the mother, family income for food, parental height, and other factors were also researched.

018. Grantham-McGregor, Sally M., and E. H. Back.
"Breastfeeding in Kingston, Jamaica." *Archives of Diseases in Children* 45:404, 1970.

This often cited study is a longitudinal study of 300 urban infants born in Kingston, Jamaica's University Hospital during the period from 1967-1968. At birth, roughly two-thirds of the infants were fed by breast alone. After six weeks the number of breastfed babies who were receiving no supplemental foods had declined to 23%. At that point a combination of breast and bottle feeding had reached 67%. The study also states that the mothers' most commonly given reason for the use of bottle feeds was lack of breast milk. In addition, the authors show a greater incidence of gastroenteritis among the bottle fed infants than in the breastfed infants.

019. Gyorgy, Paul.
"Biochemical Aspects [of Breastfeeding]." *American Journal of Clinical Nutrition* 24:970, August 1971.

This highly technical study discusses the nutritional content of human milk and contrasts it with the content of cow's milk. The author explains the differences fully. Some he considers to be quite important, for example, the presence in human milk of cystine and the presence in cow's milk of methionine which a premature infant is not able to use. The article is useful for helping the researcher to understand the technical differences between the two kinds of milk. The policy implications of the author's findings are unclear.

020. Hanafy, M., et al.
"Infant Feeding in the U.A.R. and Developing Countries." *Pakistan Pediatrics Journal,* 1970.

Although the authors favor breast milk as the best choice for infants, they recognize that significant progress has been made in artificial feeding. Breastfeeding for several months is said to be the current practice in Egypt among rural and non-working mothers. Such a practice is sanctioned by traditional Moslem teaching. The authors also say that breast milk is not "free" because extra food is required for the lactating mother. Improvement of breast milk production should begin with improving the nutrition of mothers.

021. Jelliffe, D. B.
"Nutrition Education in the Maternity Ward." *West Indian Medical Journal* 20:177, 1971.

This study of feeding practices in the English-speaking Caribbean reveals that more than 27% of the mothers had not yet decided what feeding patterns they would adopt while in the hospital: about 6% would feed on demand from the breast and about 28% would feed from the breast four or five times daily. The study contains other information about complementary feeding, types of milks used, mixing of the formula and sterilization of teats and feeding bottles.

022. Jelliffe, D. B.
"The Uniqueness of Human Milk." *American Journal of Clinical Nutrition* 24:968, 1971.

This publication is the result of a symposium on the uniqueness of breast milk. The contributors increase the knowledge of nutritionists and health workers concerning the new advances in the field of human milk research. The articles cover the questions of host resistance to infection, breastfeeding convenience, and the economic and psychological aspects of breastfeeding.

023. Kanaaneh, Hatim.
"The Relationship of Bottle Feeding to Malnutrition and Gastroenteritis in a Pre-Industrial Setting." *Environmental Child Health* December 1972.

In three pre-industrial Arabic villages in Israel, the feeding habits of two groups of children were studied. Those children experiencing the greatest health problems were those whose feeding patterns were most unrelated to breastfeeding, although the samples and categories for this study were extremely limited and, therefore, open to question. For instance, only two children received breast milk exclusive of other types of feed for the entire six month period. All others received varying combinations of breast milk, goat's milk, reconstituted tinned milk, and so forth.

024. Martinez, C. and A. Chavez.
"Nutrition and Development in Infants of Poor Rural Areas: #1. Consumption of Mother's Milk by Infants." *Nutrition Reports International* 4:139, 1971.

This article explains infant feeding practices in rural Mexico. Breastfeeding predominates until the child seeks supplemental foods at approximately eight months.

025. Mata, L. J., et al.
"Influence of Recurrent Infections on Nutrition and Growth of Children in Guatemala." *American Journal of Clinical Nutrition* 25:1267, 1972.

From 1964 to 1970 the birth weight and growth rate of infants were studied and the data evaluated. Growth retardation occurred at birth, and often continued through infancy into the pre-school years. Intrauterine infections, poor maternal nutrition, low quality weaning foods, and other childhood infections all contributed to deficits in weight.

026. McKigney, John I.
"Cost/Value and Selection of Milks for Use in Artificial Feeding." *West Indian Medical Journal* 20:213, 1971.

Twenty-two milk products widely marketed in the West Indies, many of which are used as infant feeds, were analyzed for calorie content and protein content and then their prices were determined as price per 1000 calories and price per 20 grams of protein delivered. The results are listed in the paper.

027. McKigney, John I.
"Economic Aspects [of Breastfeeding]." *American Journal of Clinical Nutrition* 24:1005, August 1971.

The author compares the costs of properly feeding a lactating mother with the costs of formula feeding. He carefully explains the various feeding regimens which could be followed. His conclusion is that there is a definite nutrient/cost advantage for breastfeeding versus bottle or formula feeding. He points out that his findings are at variance with other findings and explains why. He does admit that the cost advantage on the weekly basis is small but points out that over a six month period the cost differences do accumulate.

028. McKigney, John I.
"Family Incomes and Nutrient Cost of Foods in the Caribbean Area." *West Indian Medical Journal* 20:139, 1971.
Various surveys carried on in the West Indies, says this article, have shown that most families in the area spend from 50% to 90% of their income on food. In terms of child nutrition this means that it would be relatively difficult for family food expenditures to increase in order to achieve better nutrition. The less expensive everyday food items often have more, or at least equivalent, nutritional value than higher priced, processed, imported items. A mixture of the two kinds of food is probably most beneficial.

029. Morris, N.
"Cultural Differences and the Feeding of Young Children in the Caribbean." *West Indian Medical Journal* 20:135, 1971.
If the government and health agencies set out to alter the patterns of maternal feeding of infants, they must take into consideration the culture and class of the persons whom they are trying to reach. If they do not, the changes which they are trying to make will not be as successful as they could be.

030. Newton, D.
"Psychologic Differences Between Breast and Bottle Feeding." *American Journal of Clinical Nutrition* 24:993, August 1971.
Unrestricted breastfeeding as practiced widely in the past brings certain psychological benefits to mothers which the token breastfeeding of modern times may not offer or may offer only in a variable way. The author explores these benefits in the article.

031. Niehoff, Arthur and Natalie Meister.
"The Cultural Characteristics of Breastfeeding: A Survey." *Environmental Child Health* p. 16, March 1972.
The authors used ethnographic material from Human Relations Area Files of the University of Southern California to analyze the breastfeeding practices and beliefs of traditional cultures. The cultures chosen were heavily Asian and Middle Eastern; however, African, South American and North American cultures were included as well as others. The study is a useful summary of breastfeeding initiation, duration and termination. The sections on the duration of breastfeeding and on supplemental feeding have a direct bearing on the formula feeding controversy.

032. Plank, S. J. and M. L. Milanesi.
"Infant Feeding and Infant Mortality in Rural Chile." *Bulletin of the World Health Organization* 48:203, 1973.
Over 1,700 mothers were interviewed in rural Chile during 1969 and 1970 about their infant feeding practices. Post-neonatal deaths were more frequent among infants who started bottle feeding in the first three months than among those exclusively breastfed during that

time. The authors acknowledge that they made no evaluation of the qualitative or quantitative deficiencies of the "bottle feeding". Also, no allowance was made for the inclusion of low-weight, high-risk infants in the bottle-fed group, when supplementary milk had been medically prescribed.

033. Protein Advisory Group of the United Nations System.
PAG Statement No. 23. July 18, 1972.
The Protein Advisory Group (PAG), a United Nations agency, convened the Paris Conference of June 1972 and subsequently issued *PAG Statement #23*. The statement recognized several important things about infant feeding in developing countries. Breast milk was said to be the optimal food for infants and usually the sole source of nutrition during the first four to six months. Supplementation of breast milk with nutritionally adequate food is necessary after four to six months. The formula industry should not discourage breastfeeding, and it should attempt to find ways of minimizing the misuse of dry and liquid preparations for feeding children and, to this end, improve labeling and the label instructions about proper and hygienic preparation.

034. Ransome-Kuti, O., W. O. Gbajumo and M. O. Olaniyan.
"Some Socio-Economic Conditions Predisposing to Malnutrition in Lagos." *Nigerian Medical Journal* 2:111, 1972.
This study is based upon the questioning of 200 mothers who had been referred to the Institute of Child Health, Lagos, Nigeria, because their children were malnourished. The practices of these mothers disclosed that they used mixed feeding; that is to say, they continued to breast-feed, even into the second year of life, but they supplemented with artificial milk and with semi-solids, usually gruels of various kinds. Measles preceded the onset of kwashiorkor in over half the cases and gastroenteritis was present in over 80% of the children.

035. Reddy, S. K.
"Artificial Feeding in Jamaica and Barbados." *West Indian Medical Journal* 20:207, 1971.
The author of this study combines results from other sources covering infant feeding practices in Jamaica and Barbados. The studies show that the water used in preparation was boiled in over 90% of the cases, and that the problem is usually with overdilution of the formula. The figures on dilution are based upon questioning mothers about how long a tin of formula lasts. Most answers showed, if the question was understood properly, that the tins were lasting too long, thus prompting the conclusion about overdilution. Other information is provided by the author about vitamin, oil and juice supplements.

036. Viteri, F. E. and R. Bressani.
"The Quality of New Sources of Protein and Their Suitability for Weanlings and Young Children." *Bulletin of the World Health Organization* 46:827, 1972.
This paper describes in technical detail the process by which several formulated protein-rich mixtures, developed to prevent protein deficiencies in vulnerable populations in the less-developed world, were tested to determine their protein quality. Most of the mixtures were suitable for children of pre-school age.

037. Wickstrom, Bo.
"Marketing of Protein-Rich Foods in Developing Countries." FAO/WHO/
UNICEF, Protein Advisory Group, Guideline No. 10, 1971.
The Protein Advisory Group of the United Nations approved at its
meeting, February of 1971, Marketing Guidelines for protein-rich food
products in developing countries. The text of the Guidelines runs to
nearly 80 pages. The text states basic marketing principles which
should be observed by developing countries for the successful introduction of new high protein foods to consumer nationals. Though the
principles are said to be suitable to both controlled and free economies,
it is clear from the Guidelines that the introduction of high protein
foods is seen as a centrally planned and evaluated project.

C. NEWS ARTICLES
See "Critic Groups" listing below for opening editorials in the *New Internationalist*.

D. CRITIC GROUPS

038. "Action Now on Baby Foods."
The New Internationalist No. 6, August 1973.
Articles and commentaries in this publication played a major part in
the development of the popular Nestle boycott campaign. This short
commentary describes the cover of the *New Internationalist* for August
1973 which shows the grave of an infant marked by a feeding bottle
and an empty tin of formula. The editorial comments that though the
mother apparently deposited them on the grave to show that she had
done the best for her child, actually, these items were the main cause
of the child's death. The tone of the remainder of the piece is similar.
Promotion has caused death, and the equation is posited as a complete
one.

039. "Milk and Murder."
The New Internationalist No. 8, October 1973.
This editorial takes a strong and strident stand against Nestle and
formula feeding. The essence of the piece is that formula companies
are inducing mothers to bottle feed which kills or maims the infants.
The promotion and sale must be stopped, it concludes.

E. CHURCH PUBLICATIONS
Church groups did not generally become active in the controversy
until later. This accounts for the absence of items under this category.

F. INFANT FOOD INDUSTRY PUBLICATIONS

040. Wolflisberg, Hans J.
A Century of Global Operations: The Flavorful World of Nestle. Princeton,
N.J.: Princeton University Press, December 1966.
The former president of "U.S. Nestle" gives a short presentation on
the history and corporate outlook of Nestle. The remarks point to a

9

company which views itself as the provider of healthful and convenient food products to the world. The speech was delivered years before the formula feeding controversy but it gives insight into why activist charges against Nestle would be regarded with such strong opposition by Nestle itself.

II. PUBLIC AWARENESS, THE POPULAR CAMPAIGN, AND THE INDUSTRY RESPONSE: 1974-1977

A. GENERAL ARTICLES AND STUDIES

041. Aykroyd, W. R.
"Is Breast Feeding Best for All Infants, Everywhere?" *Nutrition Today* January/February, 1977.
This discussion by the former director of a United Nations agency raises certain important questions about the feeding of formula to infants in less-developed countries. The decline in infant mortality in the developed world over the last 60-70 years resulted from a combination of factors such as improved sanitation, better water supplies, greater safety of milk sold at retail, the infant welfare movement, and others. The author points out that the increasing use of processed cows' milk and decreasing infant mortality have coincided in affluent countries during the past century. The article states that the libel action brought by Nestle against an activist group left most of the questions about the alleged dangers of formula unanswered.

042. Bader, Michael B.
"Breast Feeding: The Role of Multinational Corporations in Latin America." *International Journal of Health and Science* 6(4):609, 1976.
This article is an early version of the concerns and objections of those opposed to formula feeding in less-developed countries. The conclusions about the decline of breastfeeding are somewhat premature given the later results of the U.N. Collaborative Study on Breastfeeding in 1979. The author makes reference to Chile as an example of a country where bottle feeding adversely affected infant health. He maintains that companies have had to increase sales in the less-developed world because their domestic markets have not expanded rapidly. He condemns the use of direct consumer advertising because it tends to discourage breastfeeding.

043. Baer, Edward.
"Infant Formula in the Lowlands." School of Management, Boston University, 1977.
This case study shows the problems facing Third World leaders as a result of the marketing of infant formula within the borders of a particular country. Prepared early in the controversy, some of the later scientific evidence is, of course, not included. Both Baer and his colleague, Post, were in the forefront of those opposed to formula feeding, and most of the sources cited are unfavorable to the industry position.

10

044. Blodgett, Timothy B. and Pamela Banks.
"Nestle: At Home Abroad: Interview with Pierre Liotard-Vogt." *Harvard Business Review* 54(6):80, November/December 1977.
This interview with the managing director of Nestle S.A. gives the reader an inside look at the managerial philosophy of Nestle in the 1970s. Nestle believes in centralized financial planning, but local choice and semi-autonomy in marketing and product introduction. Liotard-Vogt emphasizes the importance of employee loyalty to Nestle. The interview is noteworthy because it reveals the "personality" of Nestle S.A.

045. Cottingham, Jane.
"The Baby Controversy: Three Years Later." *Ideas and Action* 5:16, May 1977.
This is a critical re-evaluation of the development of the controversy from the time of its inception and is primarily hostile toward Nestle.

046. Frank, A. and S. Frank.
"Breastfeeding vs. Bottlefeeding." *Mademoiselle* 82:110, September 1976.
This article, intended for U.S. mothers, emphasizes that the choice of breastfeeding versus bottle feeding is a complex one; both methods of feeding have advantages and disadvantages. In the West, the choice should be the mother's after she has considered the options carefully.

047. Gomm, R.
"Breast — Best or Bestial?" *Midwife, Health Visitor & Community Nurse* 12:317, 1976.
The author argues that increasing dedication to natural foods and the cult of the natural among middle-class women may account for much of the movement by these groups back to breastfeeding. Professionals should guard against endorsement of the view that breastfeeding is always best.

048. Helsing, S. E.
"Women's Liberation and Breastfeeding." *Environmental Child Health* p. 290, October 1975.
The major portion of this article is devoted to an explanation of how modern women are freed from the uncertainty of child bearing which, in the past, made them less able to become part of the work force. The last portion is a presentation of the writer's attitude toward breastfeeding. She seems to favor the choice that each woman makes after she has carefully considered the evidence. Her examples appear to show her distaste for making mothers feel guilty either because they breastfeed or because they do not.

049. Hewson, Barbara.
"Influencing Multinational Corporations: The Infant Formula Marketing Controversy." *N.Y.U. International Law and Politics* Vol. 10, No. 1.
This article on the relationship of the marketing controversy to issues

in international law concludes that the controversy cannot be resolved within the purview of any existing international legal codes.

050. "Is Breast-Feeding Best for Babies?"
Consumer Reports p. 152, March 1977.
This article compares breastfeeding with formula feeding of infants. The possible contamination of human milk by the ingestion of PCB's (polychlorinated biphenyls) by mothers is not seen as a proven threat to health. The chemical make-up of cow's milk is different from human milk even though formula derived from cow's milk is modified. Breastfeeding should be tried by new mothers. Nevertheless, in developed countries, formula feeding is a satisfactory alternative to breastfeeding.

051. Kuhn, James W.
"The Role of the Market in Infant Nutrition: The Role of Nestle in Infant Formula." Columbia University, c. 1978.
In this unpublished paper, apparently written in the fall of 1978, the author reviews the beginnings of the Nestle controversy. In addition to the early decisions made by Nestle, the positions of Abbott Laboratories and Bristol-Myers are discussed. Although the paper ends with the summer of 1978, it is useful for its discussion of the initial phase of the controversy.

052. Nerlove, Sara.
"Women's Workload and Infant Feeding Practices: A Relationship with Demographic Implications." *Ethnology* 13(2):207, 1974.
This discussion of various studies on the subject of women and work and its impact upon child raising suggests that women's participation in the subsistence economy may foster higher rates of mortality and morbidity among infants and may foster higher fertility, contrary to other studies cited.

053. Raphael, Dana.
The Tender Gift: Breast Feeding. New York: Schocken Books, 1976.
A leading anthropologist encourages, with this volume, a reasoned return to breastfeeding. Dr. Raphael suggests the use of a supportive person, the mother's mother, for example, who will make it easier for the mother to give attention to her newborn. Dr. Raphael carefully explains the process of lactation and, in addition, gives a brief history of how American mothers gradually departed from breastfeeding in the early twentieth century. The book provides insight into the "back to breastfeeding literature" which kindled many women's groups dedicated to ending formula feeding.

054. Sethi, S. P.
"Dimensions of Corporate Social Performance . . . ." *California Management Review* p. 58, Spring 1975.
Sethi tries to provide a set of criteria by which to assess the social responsibility of corporate enterprises over periods of time. His article states that too often the phrase "corporate social responsibility" is ambiguous. Terms like "legitimacy", however, used by the writer in his discussion, do not seem to have much concrete identification. The

piece is used and referred to by others writing about the formula feeding controversy.

055. Sethi, S. P. and J. E. Post.
"Marketing of Infant Formula Food in Less Developed Countries: Some Public Consequences of Private Action." Center for Research in Business and Social Policy, School of Management, University of Texas at Dallas, c. 1977.
This study places the formula feeding controversy in the context of multinational companies selling Western products into less-developed countries. The study asks the questions: To what extent should a business firm be responsible for the unintended results of the use of its products? Under what circumstances should greater self-restraint be used in the promotion of products? The authors use the formula feeding controversy as a specific case. They present the history of the industry, industry business strategy, and other background information. Industry promotion practices and a criticism of these practices are also presented. The authors then propose a framework by which to analyze the practices of the industry. They refer to the pre-problem stage, the identification stage, the remedy and relief stage, and the prevention stage.

056. Terpstra, Vern.
"Case 12-3 — Nestle Alimentana, S.A.: Can Advertising Be a Killer?" In: International Marketing, 2nd ed. Hinsdale, IL: The Dryden Press, 1977; p. 438.
This study is presented in an international marketing book. Many graduate and undergraduate students would come into contact with the issue in this manner. Since the case is dated 1977, it focuses on the libel action brought by Nestle against the Swiss activist group for its publication of a pamphlet entitled "Nestle Kills Babies". The appendix to the case contains a press statement made by Nestle's Managing Director, Dr. Arthur Furer, who recognizes the possible problems with purchases of formula by some Third World mothers. He points out the efforts being made by Nestle to educate against improper use. He counsels greater attention to the general problems of unsanitary conditions in less-developed countries.

057. Wickstrom, Bo.
"Report on an Investigation of Infant Food Companies in Europe and the United States and Their Policies for Marketing in the Developing World." The Infant Food Marketing Study; A Sub-Project to WHO/CIE Collaborative Study on Breast-Feeding", Goteborg, April 1977.
The body of this report presents information and analysis of the marketing of infant formula by some fifteen European and United States' firms. The author adopts a model of innovation production and reception as his basic scheme. Under this approach infant formula is seen as an innovation and the question is whether the innovation producers (business firms) see to it that the new product goes to a segment of receivers (consumers) who have the purchasing power to buy it, need it, and will not be likely to use it improperly. The author conducted interviews with 35 officials of 15 European and American firms asking them 16 main questions about marketing organization and corrective action if improper marketing was found. Many quotations from the questionnaire are of interest. On the whole, specific

questions about market size were not answered. The author favors a better targeting of consumers — sometimes called segmented marketing — in order to limit the sale of formula to the poor and semi-literate.

B. SCIENTIFIC ARTICLES AND STUDIES

058. Addy, D. P.
"Infant Feeding: A Current View." *British Medical Journal* 1:1268, 1976. The author gives his reasons for opposing artificial feeding and concludes that the following potentially harmful developments "incriminate" artificial feeding: gastrointestinal infections, cow's milk allergies, obesity and others. The piece is intended to give advice to modern mothers in Britain.

059. Behar, M.
"The Role of Feeding and Nutrition in the Pathogeny and Prevention of Diarrheic Processes." *Bulletin of the Pan Am Health Organization* 9:1, 1975. One of the central issues in the formula feeding controversy is the relationship between breastfeeding and the prevention of bacterial infections which generate diarrhea. This study furnishes data from Guatemala about the protection which breastfeeding provides against such gastrointestinal infections. The author also notes that vulnerability to diarrhea is increased by malnutrition.

060. Berg, Alan.
"The Crisis in Infant Feeding Practices." *Nutrition Today,* January/February 1977.
Nutrition planner Berg says that less-developed countries in which breastfeeding has declined are losing a valuable natural resource when their mothers abandon traditional patterns of nursing and shift to artificial feeds. Berg explains the reasons for the superiority of breast milk over artificial formulas and names various causes which have contributed to the decline of breastfeeding, particularly in urban areas. Among those causes recognized by Berg are: urbanization and modernization, changing social attitudes (such as those of the woman toward her appearance and toward being free of the constraints of breastfeeding), the existence of advertising claims, and the easy availability of skim milk from institutional feeding programs. Berg advocates the dissemination of information about the benefits of breastfeeding and the drawbacks of artificial feeding. He also believes that governmental limits on advertising and on commercial access to health care facilities are needed.

061. Brown, J. E. and R. C. Brown.
"Finding the Causes of Protein-Calorie Malnutrition in a Community." *Journal of Tropical Pediatrics* 23:248, Monograph #51, 1977.
Preventing the malnutrition of infants in less-developed countries is the aim of the papers which make up this monograph. After designing a method of identifying causes of malnutrition, its practical application was made in Bulape, Zaire. Researchers found that infant food was available, but the choice of food and the feeding were inadequate. Mothers who worked in agriculture would often nurse only before leaving and after returning from work. In the meantime, the infant

was fed low quality gruel made from grain or cassava. Various recurring problems were identified and solutions proposed.

062. Center for Science in the Public Interest.
"White Paper on Infant Feeding Practices." C.S.P.I., Citizens Committee on Infant Nutrition, Washington, D.C., 1974.
The paper states that although commercial formulas are acceptable substitutes for human milk, certain advantages of breastfeeding have not yet been duplicated by modern technology. The advantages include the anti-infective properties of breast milk and the close bonding of infant and mother fostered by breastfeeding.

063. Chavez, A., et al.
"Child Nutrition Problems During Lactation in Poor Rural Areas." In: *Proceedings of IXth International Congress of Nutrition, Mexico, 1972.* Basel: S. Karger, 1975; 2:90.
The lactation performance of rural Mexican mothers who received supplemental food, including milk protein, vitamins, iron and minerals, was higher in volume for the first six months of production than a comparable unsupplemented control group. After six months, however, output of the supplemented mothers declined so that when the concentration of solids produced was compared, production was similar between supplemented and unsupplemented groups.

064. CIBA Foundation Symposium 45.
Breastfeeding and the Mother. Amsterdam: Associated Scientific Publisher, 1976. (or New York: Elsevier Publishers, 1976.)
This collection of papers from a symposium on the subject of "Breastfeeding and the Mother" contains many useful articles about the physiology of breastfeeding, such as the hormonal control of lactation, maternal nutrition and lactation, and the psychology of lactation. The book closes with chapters on cultural and social aspects of breastfeeding.

065. Crawford, M. A., B. M. Laurence and A. E. Munhambo.
"Breastfeeding and Human Milk Composition." *Lancet* i:99, 1977.
East African mothers whose children failed to grow appropriately while being breastfed had a low lipid content to their breast milk. Milk tests suggested low fat content and inadequate lipid synthesis from carbohydrates.

066. Crow, Rosemary A.
"An Ethological Study of the Development of Infant Feeding." *Journal of Advanced Nursing* 2:99, 1977.
The author, by using the approach of careful observation of nursing mothers and bottle feeding mothers, identifies five areas where faulty feeding may occur. For example, the concept of feeding may be incorrect, or the feeding technique may be improper, or the feedback provided by the child may be misunderstood by the mother. All these areas may lead to faulty feeding.

067. Cunningham, Alan.
"Morbidity in Breast Fed and Artificially Fed Infants." *Journal of Pediatrics* 90(5):726, May 1977.
Breastfed infants experienced less illness than did their bottle fed

counterparts according to this study conducted in a rural community in New York. Breastfeeding was begun by 50% of the mothers. At the end of one year the proportion of breastfeeding had declined to 4%.

068. Davies, D. P.
"Adequacy of Expressed Breast Milk for Early Growth of Preterm Infants." *Archives of Disease in Children* 52:296, 1977.
Fourteen preterm infants (28-32 weeks) who received artificial formula (Ostermilk 1) achieved greater growth in length, head circumference and weight than a similar control group which received pooled mature breast milk. For more mature preterm infants (33-36 weeks) no difference of statistical significance was noted. Variation in protein needs and intake of the groups may account for the differences in growth.

069. Eastham, E., et al.
"Further Decline in Breast Feeding." *British Medical Journal* 1(6005):305, February 7, 1976.
The writers employed structured interviews to survey mothers who chose to breastfeed and mothers who chose to bottle feed. The primary reason for their decisions was past experience defined as their own personal experience or that of their family and friends. The fact that many mothers prematurely stopped breastfeeding limited accessability of more technical information about breastfeeding.

070. Edozien, J. C., M. A. R. Khan and C. I. Waslien.
"Human Protein Deficiency: Results of a Nigerian Village Study." *Journal of Nutrition* 106:312, 1976.
The major conclusion of this study is that the feeding of supplemental skimmed milk to lactating mothers had the effect of raising the protein content of their diet and then increasing the volume of milk that they were able to produce for their nursing children.

071. Eide, W. B.
"Women in Food Production, Food Handling and Nutrition." *PAG Bulletin* 7:40, 1977.
The agricultural labor foce in less-developed countries is higher as a percentage than in the developed world. Women often compose a high percentage of agricultural workers. The author points out that in Africa, women make up from 60% to 80% of the farm or agricultural labor force. Nutritionists promoting breastfeeding to such female agricultural workers must remember the practical obstacles presented by their occupations.

072. Fomon, S. J. and L. J. Filer, Jr.
Infant Nutrition. 2nd ed. Saunders, 1974.
In chapter 15 (p. 359) of this work the authors discuss "Milks and Formula." They first present information about the composition of human milk, such as the presence of colostrom, vitamins, minerals and enzymes in the milk. Cow's milk is compared with human milk. Foreign substances in human milk in modern societies are catalogued. Here attention is given to the presence of lead and pesticides. Milk-based and soya-based formulas are then analyzed.

073. Greiner, Ted.

"The Promotion of Bottle Feeding by Multinational Corporations: How Advertising and the Health Professions Have Contributed." In: *Cornell International Nutrition Monograph Series No. 2.* Ithaca, N.Y.: Cornell University, 1975.

The author studied much of the literature, including ads, booklets and other materials, prepared by the formula companies which sell their products in low income areas of the world. The promotional literature was then rated according to different criteria. For example, the number of pages devoted to promoting breastfeeding as opposed to formula feeding was counted. The number of positive and negative statements about various kinds of feeding was tabulated. The writer concludes that the promotional literature was anti-breastfeeding on the whole. Some of the advertising copy in this report is very old — 1916, 1939.

074. Greiner, Ted.

"Regulation and Education: Strategies for Solving the Bottle Feeding Problem." In: *Cornell International Nutrition Monograph Series No. 4.* Ithaca, N.Y.: Cornell University, 1975.

Early in the controversy this study by Greiner maintained that formula feeding was a severe problem in less-developed countries because its improper use created contamination and infection, thereby aggravating malnutrition. The work mentions urbanization and changing culture as reasons for shifting from breast to bottle, but primarily attributes the use of bottle feeding to the promotional activities of formula companies. The report does not mention the later efforts of formula companies to curtail direct consumer advertising. Many consumer ads are included as part of the study.

075. Habicht, J. P., et al.

"Repercussions of Lactation on Nutritional Status of Mother and Infant." In: *Proceedings of the IXth International Congress of Nutrition, Mexico, 1972.* Basel: S. Karger, 1975; 2:106.

The authors suggest that Guatemalean mothers who had low weight gains during their pregnancy ceased to lactate after three months because lactation tends to decline at a certain weight deficit to protect the mother from health-damaging weight loss. The authors also state that families with working mothers may desire greater family income resulting in the mother's return to work and purchasing of artificial formulas.

076. Hakim, P. and G. Solimano.

"Supplemental Feeding as a Nutritional Intervention: The Chilean Experience in the Distribution of Milk." *Journal of Tropical Pediatrics* 22:185, 1976.

From 1924 through the mid-1970s, the Chilean government engaged in a milk distribution program. The organizational cost and educational efforts of the program are discussed. The Chilean program has been criticized for discouraging breastfeeding and actually worsening the conditions of infants, but the authors present evidence that breastfeeding had already been declining before the program reached its peak and that infant deaths and malnutrition declined during the height of the program.

077. The Human Lactation Center.
"Mothers in Poverty: Breastfeeding and the Maternal Struggle for Infant Survival." *The Lactation Review* 2(3), 1977.

This report takes the position that poverty in general is the single most important cause of poor infant health and low survival rates. Mere encouragement of increased breastfeeding cannot be expected to improve infant health absent efforts to improve water supplies and other sanitary facilities. The author advocates the encouragement of "mixed feeding" which means breastfeeding supplemented by artificial feeds beginning at about four to six months. Other supportive measures, such as educational programs, media campaigns, etc., are necessary to further the success of the mother in infant feeding.

078. Intengan, C. L.
"Nutritional Evaluation of Breastfeeding Practices in Some Countries of the Far East," *Journal of Tropical Pediatrics* 22:63, 1976.

Using data from certain Far Eastern countries, the author states that a growing decline in breastfeeding exists among urbanized, Westernized affluent women. Insufficient milk, employment and a second pregnancy were among the reasons proffered for stopping breastfeeding. Advertising and marketing by formula companies have also contributed to the decline in breastfeeding.

079. Intengan, C. L.
"Nutritional Evaluation of Breastfeeding Practices in the Far East." *Environmental Child Health* p. 63, April 1976.

Breastfeeding has been deeply rooted in the Far East. Some mothers have held the view that any other supplemental food is detrimental during breastfeeding. The widely accepted position now, however, is that after five to six months some supplementation is needed. Unfortunately some infants do not receive this mixed feeding but receive only formula from the beginning. These are the children who suffer the most from protein-energy malnutrition. The author also discusses the trend in infant feeding as well as urbanization and its effects on traditional feeding practices. According to Intengan, greater efforts need to be made to encourage breastfeeding.

080. Jelliffe, D. B.
"Community and Socio-Political Considerations of Breastfeeding." In: CIBA Foundation Symposium 45. *Breastfeeding and the Mother.* New York: Elsevier Publishers, 1976; p. 231.

Western cultural attitudes tend to make successful lactation more difficult. These attitudes cause anxiety in the mother and thus inhibit normal lactation. Among the attitudes mentioned are: Western overvaluing of manufactured products, women's breasts seen as erotic objects rather than as a means of nurturing, and commercial pressure and goals being passed on to consumers. These attitudes must be changed in order to improve the likelihood of breastfeeding. The change can be accomplished by education and by regulatory legislation, says this author.

081. Jelliffe, D. B.
"World Trends in Infant Feeding." *American Journal of Clinical Nutrition* 29:1227, November 1976.

The author sets forth three "planks" for sound, scientifically guided infant feeding. The first plank is to feed the pregnant and lactating mothers with a mixed diet of locally available foods. The second plank is to breastfeed exclusively for four to six months. The last plank is to introduce the least costly weaning foods from four to six months onward, preferably from local sources with continuing lactation even into the second year. Jelliffe explains that human milk has unique characteristics. He decries inappropriate and misleading advertising of infant formula, and he complains that health professionals frequently show little interest in issues of nutrition. The author estimates that a widespread return to breastfeeding would "protect" some 10 million infants each year who are affected by marasmus and diarrheal diseases.

082. Jelliffe, D. B. and E. F. P. Jelliffe.
"Breast Is Best: Modern Meanings." *New England Journal of Medicine* 297:912, October 27, 1977.
In this article the writers advocate programs for promoting increased breastfeeding to counter the claimed harmful effects of an increase in bottle feeding. The benefits of breastfeeding are reviewed and the charge is made against the infant formula industry and against organized medicine that too much attention and effort have been given to artificial feeding to the detriment of breastfeeding, a much better and generally safer method.

083. Jelliffe, D. B. and E. F. P. Jelliffe.
"Human Milk in the Modern World: An Overview." *American Journal of Clinical Nutrition* 24:1013, August 1977.
The well-known advocates of breastfeeding review the biochemical properties of breast milk, the emotional and maternal advantages of breastfeeding, and the need for better technical and general education about breastfeeding.

084. Jelliffe, D. B. and E. F. P. Jelliffe.
"Human Milk, Nutrition and the World Resource Crisis." *Science* 188:557, May 9, 1975.
This early piece by two of the most important, consistent supporters of breastfeeding raises certain issues which several years later became the center of the formula feeding controversy. This article explains the particular benefits of breastfeeding in the battle against protein-calorie malnutrition which is fought each day in many Third World countries. Breast milk has anti-infective properties, helps in child spacing, and is economically cheaper than any other form of nutrition for the child. This early article features nearly all the issues that are eventually raised in the formula controversy.

085. Kevaney, J., et al.
"Influences on Choice of Infant Feeding Methods." *Irish Medical Journal* 68:499, 1975.
Over 80% of mothers in four Dublin, Ireland hospitals artificially fed infants following birth. The frequency of artificial feeding in the previous generation was 35%. Other information about the lack of availability to first-time mothers of support and information led the

authors to advocate better education of mothers by health care professionals.

086. Laditan, A. A. O. and P. J. Reeds.
"A Study of the Age of Onset, Diet and the Importance of Infection in the Pattern of Severe Protein-energy Malnutrition in Ibadan, Nigeria." *British Journal of Nutrition* 36:411, 1976.
Protein-energy malnutrition is the subject of this study by doctors in Nigeria. Their patients were infants who had been breastfed for at least nine months. Supplemental feedings were usually made with maize-starch gruels. Measles and gastrointestinal infections were common. The authors recommend, among other things, immunizations against measles.

087. Lambert, J. and J. Basford.
"Port Moresby Infant Feeding Survey." *Papua New Guinea Medical Journal* 20:175, 1977.
This study compares the nutritional status of infants who were breastfed with those who were artificially fed. Of those who were below 80% of weight for age, 26% were breastfed and 69% were artificially fed. No information is provided about relative birth weights of the two groups.

088. Latham, M. C.
"Infant Feeding in National and International Perspective." *Annals New York Academy of Sciences* 300:197, 1977.
Latham divides the world into three unequal groups — countries where breastfeeding remains the principal means of feeding, countries where bottle feeding is the principal means used, and countries which are in transition from breast to bottle feeding. Latham says that there is, in general, a correlation between capitalism and bottle feeding as well as a correlation between socialism and breastfeeding. The evidence on this point is of poor quality and is not convincing. The author does provide some data which favor breastfeeding in less-developed countries for economic reasons. The article advocates breastfeeding, but if a country's mothers have clearly chosen formula feeding over breasfeeding, then Latham favors subsidization of the formula in order to keep down costs to users.

089. Lindblad, B. S., et al.
"The Composition and Yield of Human Milk in Developing Countries." *XIIIth Symposium of the Swedish Nutrition Foundation* p. 125, 1977.
By reviewing studies from developing countries like India, Egypt and others, plus their own studies, the authors conclude that living conditions in poor areas may adversely affect the quantity of milk output.

090. Margulies, Leah.
"A Critical Essay on the Role of Promotion in Bottle Feeding." *PAG Bulletin* 7:73, 1977.
The writer asserts that because domestic markets were saturated, formula companies sought markets in less-developed countries for infant formula and related products. She maintains that health care workers, including physicians, agree to allow samples of the products

to be distributed in hospitals because they want the extra equipment which the formula companies buy for them. The article also describes the activities of milk nurses who are company representatives said to be promoting formula feeding. The author calls for discontinuance of promotion of formula and greater governmental regulation of related areas.

091. Mata, L. J. and J. J. Urrutia.
"Infections and Infectious Diseases in a Malnourished Population: A Long Term Prospective Field Study." *XIIIth Symposium of the Swedish Nutrition Foundation* p. 42, 1977.
This study records the results of infant feeding practices in the village of Santa Maria Cauque. Infants were breastfed for two to three months, then gruels of cereal, rice and starch were introduced. Weaning was completed on the mode of about 22 months. The article contains much technical information about the effects of breastfeeding on the child's resistance to infection.

092. Omer, H. A., M. I. A. Omer and O. O. Khalifa.
"Pattern of Protein-Energy Malnutrition in Sudanese Children and Comparison with Some Other Middle East Countries." *Journal of Tropical Pediatrics* 21:329, 1975.
This study of 119 malnourished children in Khartoum between May and December 1973 shows that although all 119 were breastfed, usually for one year, inadequate supplementary feeding and gastrointestinal infections contributed to their malnourishment.

093. Omololu, A.
"The Importance of Breastfeeding in Nigeria." Paper presented at a Seminar/ Workshop on Breastfeeding. Lagos, August 1977.
The author states that breastfeeding has declined in Nigeria. Unfortunately many mothers have improperly prepared milk substitutes and this in turn has produced marasmus and gastroenteritis. Promotional sales and health professionals are criticized for contributing to this trend.

094. Orwell, S. and J. Murray.
"Infant Feeding and Health in Ibadan." *Environmental Child Health* p. 206, August 1974.
The authors studied the feeding practices of Ibadan, Nigeria mothers. Their conclusions are varied and well-presented. Breastfeeding as the exclusive source of feeding was on the decline. Only one out of 500 mothers, on the other hand, used formula exclusively due to its high cost. Ninety-five percent of mothers used combinations of breast and bottle feeding and believed that they had been advised to do so by doctors or health workers. The most frequently used weaning food was diluted pap or ogi. Also, the authors found that fathers played an important role in the choice and purchase of food and medicine.

095. Orwell, S. and J. Murray.
"Infant Feeding and Health in Ibadan." *Journal of Tropical Pediatrics* 20:206, Monograph #35, 1974.
This study, with no methodology given, represents the results of a

study of Nigerian infant feeding practices. Other studies are mentioned, but the authors' own study of 500 mothers in Ibadan disclosed that breastfeeding was universal although supplementary bottle feeding was common within the first three months.

096. Robbin-Coker, D. J. O. and M. A. S. Jalloh.
"Infant Feeding and Protein-Calorie Malnutrition in Freetown." *Journal of Tropical Pediatrics* 21:14, 1975.
In the West African country of Sierra Leone at a hospital in the large city of Freetown, the authors studied the infants admitted with protein-energy malnutrition. A large percentage of the infants under one year of age had not been breastfed. Increased use of breast milk substitutes is attributed to urbanization, monogamy, and employment of women. Mothers with higher education and income can successfully prepare and pay for formula. Mothers with lower incomes or those with little sanitary knowledge are more likely to feed their children contaminated or overly diluted formula.

097. Rowland, M. G. M. and J. P. K. McCollum.
"Malnutrition and Gastroenteritis in the Gambia." *Transactions of the Royal Society of Tropical Medicine & Hygiene* 71:199, 1977.
In Keneba, Gambia gastroenteritis reached its peak in infants at nine months of age. The prevalence of gastroenteritis is due, in part, to the contamination of well water. Infant foods, mostly gruels, contained unacceptably high levels of bacterial contamination. Abnormal bacterial counts were found in small intestine aspirates in three-fourths of the cases.

098. "The Rural Kenyan Nutrition Survey, February-March 1977."
Social Perspectives. Central Bureau of Statistics, Ministry of Finance and Planning, Government of Kenya, September 1977.
This long and thorough report by the government of Kenya on the subject of infant feeding of some 1400 children contains very helpful data. Breastfeeding as the exclusive source of nutrients is not sufficient for the infant past six months. One conclusion is that the inferred lack of supplementary foods for children nursing for prolonged periods seems to be a more severe nutritional problem than early weaning. Extensive tables of data are available.

099. Sjolin, S.
"Present Trends in Breastfeeding," *Current Medical Research Opinions* 4:17, Suppl. 1, 1976.
This article posits the thesis that early support and encouragement by hospital personnel can play an important role in cultivating positive attitudes of mothers toward breastfeeding. The author points out that hospital practices of weighing infants immediately before and after breastfeeding were discontinued because it put mothers under unnecessary anxiety. Better information about breastfeeding is also a necessary part of the education program to encourage breastfeeding.

100. Sjolin, S., Y. Hofvander and C. Hillervik.
"Factors Related to Early Termination of Breast Feeding: A Retrospective Study in Sweden." *Acta Paediatrica Scandinavica* 66:505, 1977.
This study in Uppsala, Sweden was made of nearly 300 mothers to

determine their reasons for discontinuing breastfeeding. In about two-thirds of the mothers who began breastfeeding, anxiety, stress and tiredness, lack of motivation, and work outside the home all played a part in the decision to stop breastfeeding. Other reasons given were inconvenience and concern for physical appearance. The authors suggest greater support for nursing mothers.

101. Spalding, E., et al.
"A Study of Severely Malnourished Children in the Gambia." *Journal of Tropical Pediatrics* 23:215, 1977.
The most common form of malnutrition observed by the medical staff of a Fajara, Gambia hospital during 1974 and 1975 was marasmus. The incidence of malnutrition and dehydration varied with the season, increasing during the rainy season, an occurrence observed by other tropical medics. The authors also say that breast milk production as it could be measured was low in mothers of malnourished children.

102. "A Swedish Code of Ethics for Marketing of Infant Foods."
Acta Paediatrica Scandinavica 66: 129, 1977.
This piece refuses to attribute the choice of formula by Third World and other mothers solely to the presence of promotional materials from the infant food industry. Instead, a multiplicity of causes are cited. In addition, the editorial warns governments that free distribution of formula by the state may have as much to do with improper use as the selling of infant formula is alleged to have caused.

103. Tarnow-Mordi, W.
"Infant Malnutrition in Africa: The Role of Artificial Milk Feeds." *Environmental Child Health* p. 239, October 1974.
Artificial feeding as shown by some studies has been on the decline in Africa, especially among the urban dwellers. The hazards of artificial feeding are infection and malnutrition. Since, however, nutritionists agree that breast milk is not sufficient as the sole source of nutriments after six months, some supplementation is necessary. Commercial formulas are expensive, so supplements should come from indigenous sources as recommended in the recipes of the Protein Advisory Group Manual designed for this purpose.

104. Taylor, B.
"Viewpoint: Breast Versus Bottle Feeding." *New Zealand Medical Journal* 85:253, 1977.
The article briefly presents the advantages of breastfeeding and proposes increased education of expectant mothers about breastfeeding along with changes in hospital management of labor to encourage more mothers to breastfeed. The author recommends breastfeeding alone for a period of from four to six months.

105. Thomson, A. M. and A. E. Black.
"Nutritional Aspects of Human Lactation." *Bulletin of the World Health Organization* 52:163, 1975.
The article concluded that even for impoverished mothers and even in communities where malnutrition is common, the average growth weight of infants can be maintained satisfactorily up to the age of

three months by the use of breastfeeding alone. Such breastfeeding should be encouraged according to these authors. After the age of three months supplementation is likely to become increasingly necessary.

106. "Viewpoint Breast Feeding: A Statement of the Infant Nutrition Subcommittee of the Pediatric Society of New Zealand." *New Zealand Medical Journal* 86(593):144, August 10, 1977.
In this article the author presents most of the known arguments against formula feeding and in favor of breastfeeding, including the positive protections which breast milk provides against certain infections, the economic costs of formula feeding, and many others.

107. Wade, N.
"Bottle Feeding: Adverse Effects of a Western Technology." *Science* 184:45, April 5, 1974; Discussion 184:937, May 31, 1974.
This is a short article written early in the controversy, well before most of the serious boycott efforts were under way. Wade's position is that bottle feeding is a waste of resources that can be ill given up by Third World mothers. Modern urban development and the advice of Western trained or influenced pediatricians are also cited as causes of the alleged increase in bottle feeding and decrease in breastfeeding. The persons quoted, such as Dr. Derrick Jelliffe, are those who have been generally in favor of breastfeeding and against formula feeding.

108. Weichert, Carol.
"Breast Feeding: First Thoughts." *Pediatrics* 56(6):987, December 1975.
The author explores the various anxieties which women who are contemplating breastfeeding experience. The woman may fear that her figure will be adversely affected, thus making her less sexually desirable, or she may believe that because she has small breasts she cannot breastfeed. These and other concerns need to be addressed by the physician if breastfeeding is to be successfully advocated. The author also sees the prevailing view of the breast as a sex object to be part of the problem of encouraging breastfeeding.

109. Whitehead, R. G.
"The Infant Food Industry." *Lancet* November 27, 1976.
This long, well-documented letter explains to readers that in less-developed countries a real need exists for infants after three months of age to have supplemental feeding. The author, in response to charges that malnutrition and disease were largely to be found where commercial feeds were widely used, refutes such a view by pointing out that gastroenteritis is a severe problem in communities where commercial infant formula and other artificial baby food are not known.

110. Wing, H. J. and Tsang Ping Ham.
"A Comparative Study of Mothers' Attitudes to Breast and Bottle Feeding at Tsan Yuk Hospital in Spring of 1976." *Bulletin of the Hong Kong Medical Association* 29:63, 1977.
This study is based upon interviews with 200 mothers in a Hong Kong hospital within two or three days after giving birth. The mothers were asked about their attitudes toward breastfeeding, it being more com-

mon in older mothers and in mothers who had given birth to children previously. Apparently the attitudes of the husband, relatives and friends played a major part in determining feeding practices. Advertisements by formula companies influenced mothers in 25% of the cases of mothers who bottle fed. Work, embarrassment and convenience were the most commonly given reasons for formula use. The figures used include under the category "breastfed" those who partially breastfeed.

C. NEWS ARTICLES

111. Barness, Lewis A.
"Breast Milk for All." *New England Journal of Medicine* 297(17):939, October 27, 1977.
This editorial in a respected medical journal takes the position that formula, although modified to be more like breast milk than untreated cow's milk, still is not as advantageous in all respects as breast milk. The dangers of formula feeding in less-developed countries is mentioned. The author wants to allow for formula feeding but says that ideally more breastfeeding should be encouraged.

112. Benderly, B. L.
"Bottle Baby Disease: Boycott of Nestle Products in an Attempt to Stop Promotion of Infant Formula in Underdeveloped Countries." *MS* 6:20, December 1977.
This one page insert summarizes one view of the controversy. Infant formula has been promoted as a modern advance, but in reality it is doing harm in the less-developed world because women there are not preparing the formula properly. The writer counsels readers of the magazine to write for information from INFACT. The interconnection of the dispute with women's concerns is evident here.

113. "Breasts, Not Bottles."
Science Digest 79:21, May 1976.
This is an unsigned news item citing an article by two Cornell nutritionists (Latham and Greiner) which argues for the superiority of breastfeeding over bottle feeding.

114. "Formula Flap: Controversy over Nestle Alimentana's Sale of Infant's Powdered Milk Formulas in Underdeveloped Areas." *Time* 107:57, February 16, 1976.
This brief news article reports the beginnings of the controversy. Quoted are minister Hans Schmocker, member of the anti-Nestle Third World Group, and Managing Director of Nestle, S.A., Arthur Furer. The libel trial which Nestle filed against the Third World groups is referred to.

115. "The Infant Food Industry."
Lancet 2(7984):503, September 4, 1976.
Early in the dispute *Lancet* comments that due to the acquiescence of the medical profession, the infant food industry has been too dominant in the molding of infant feeding practices. The commentary refers to the libel suit brought by Nestle in Switzerland and to the issuance of other anti-Nestle literature.

116. "Milk Marketers in LDCs Change Sales in Response to Attacks." *Business International* p. 323, October 8, 1976.

This brief news article reports on the responses of formula companies to challenges by critic groups that assert that the marketing of infant formula in less-developed countries is misleading and confusing to native consumers. Companies are curtailing and reassessing their marketing practices including the use of "milk nurses", product instructions and advertising.

D. CRITIC GROUPS

117. Astrachan, A.
"Milking the Third World: Manufactured Milk vs. Breastfeeding." *Progressive* 40:34, July 1976.

The author produces one of the earliest pieces which clearly opposes the position of the formula feeding industry. He accepts the general view that multinational companies cause frequent and considerable harm to the peoples of Third World countries. The author gives attention to the libel suit brought by Nestle against the Third World Working Group and amply paraphrases David Cox, President of Ross Laboratories, whose company adopted a code of its own rather than join with the members of ICIFI. Quoted are Muller's "The Baby Killer" and Dr. D. B. Jelliffe, supporter of breastfeeding.

118. Dobrin, Lyn.
"The Scandal." *Food Monitor* 1:8, September 1977.

This essay recounts a number of instances in which Third World mothers used bottles to feed their babies after which the babies died. Whether they died from some factor related to the bottle feeding is not clear. The piece passionately opposes bottle feeding.

119. Garson, Barbara.
"The Bottle Baby Scandal: Milking the Third World for All It's Worth." *Mother Jones* p. 33, December 1977.

As the title would imply, this is a classic summary of the attack on the firms selling infant formula. Also emphasized is the trend toward bottle feeding and away from breastfeeding.

120. Infant Formula Action Coalition.
"Boycott Nestle Taster's Choice — Save a Baby's Life." Minneapolis: INFACT, undated.

This pamphlet, published by Infant Formula Action Coalition (INFACT), makes the claim that between one and three million infants have died as a result of being improperly bottle fed. The pamphlet shows an emaciated child with the caption: "Crimes Like These Demand a Boycott!" The flier illustrates the strident tone of the popular INFACT campaign.

121. Interfaith Center on Corporate Responsibility.
"Breast vs. Bottle: The Scientific Evidence of Breastfeeding." NY: ICCR, undated.

This article contains a series of single paragraph quotations from a variety of scholarly sources. Those selected are uniformly favorable to breastfeeding. In contrasting breastfeeding with bottle feeding, the quotations do not make clear whether bottle feeding necessarily means just commercial formula or if it includes the feeding of native preparations by bottle.

122. Johnson, Doug.
"Weaning Nestle From the Third World." *Food Monitor* p. 12, September 1977.
By means of this open letter to the President of U.S. Nestle, Mr. Johnson explains the boycott strategy, disagrees with the effects of the libel action, and sets out the initial demands of the critic groups. He demands that mass media advertising, milk nurses, sampling and promotion to health professionals be discontinued.

123. "Kicking the Bottle."
New Internationalist No. 25, May 1975.
The writers of the article take credit for calling the baby food "scandal" to the world's attention during 1973. They excoriate Nestle for its response to date and urge others to join in the effort to stop its promotional campaigns and the disastrous consequences which follow from it. According to this article, babies are still being stunted because of Nestle's activities.

124. Margulies, Leah.
"Cracks in the Bottle." *New Internationalist* April 1977.
The author sets out a brief case against each of several infant food firms: American Home Products, Bristol-Myers, Nestle, Borden, and Abbott. The writer stresses the harm that promotion of the product creates in the less-developed world. Baby food action groups were cropping up, according to the article, in various United States cities. Seen here is a gathering storm of dissatisfaction and protest which eventually turns into the Nestle boycott.

125. Margulies, Leah.
"Notes from Venezuela and Jamaica: Bottle Feeding Problems Persist." *The Corporate Examiner* 6:2, November 1977.
In this editorial the writer reports on a recent trip to Venezuela and Jamaica during which her visits with hospital personnel and physicians convinced her that bottle feeding in unsanitary conditions leads to health problems and that the distribution of infant formula is a major factor in the bottle feeding trend.

126. Margulies, Leah.
"Sisters of the Precious Blood." *Food Monitor* 1:10, September 1977.
The writer reports that the suit brought by an Ohio-based religious order, Sisters of the Precious Blood, has been dismissed, though it is under appeal. The order sued Bristol-Myers for its response to a shareholder resolution concerning the firm's sale of infant formula in the less-developed world.

127. Muller, Mike.
"Money, Milk, and Marasmus." *New Scientist* February 18, 1974.
The author, who later wrote the famous report indicting bottle feeding,

explains what he sees as a trend away from breastfeeding in the less-developed world. Muller favors breastfeeding because it is potentially less dangerous than bottle feeding. He cites Nestle's view that infant formula should not come into the picture in most cases until after successful breastfeeding. He also says that Nestle favors the distribution of formula through health workers, yet Nestle directly promotes the products. PAG Statement #23 is often cited. Overall the tone is calm and the proposals are directed to governments to alert them to the possible problems of artificial feeding.

128. Muller, Mike.
"The Baby Killer." A War on Want Investigation into the Promotion and Sale of Powdered Baby Milks in the Third World. London: War on Want, March 1974.
This report is a catalogue of charges against formula feeding practices in the Third World. The Muller report uses language that is at times quite blunt. For example, the choice of infant formula is said to be a choice of disease rather than health. Other portions of the report are temperate in tone and analysis. Muller does quote nutritionists who work for Nestle and other companies and often includes their statements. The report is one of the most important and oft-quoted in the controversy. It is fair to say that Muller's report launched the popular campaign against Nestle even though other groups had taken it up previously.

129. Ritchie, Mark.
Speech Reprint. Minneapolis: INFACT, April 1977.
Mr. Ritchie, with the organization, Earthwork, addressed the Northern California chapter of INFACT. His remarks are interesting because they help the researcher to understand that the Nestle boycott is seen by some boycotters as a part of a larger movement to call corporate capitalism to account. Ritchie regards himself and others in the boycott as victims of the corporate class which is organizing the world for their own interests. He gives his version of the launching of the 1977 boycott of Nestle products. He reveals that the activists chose an issue which had appeal and a boycott which would feature commonly used products. For those interested in media, Ritchie points out that the organizers of the boycott were well aware that people generally do not read. Therefore, if any campaign of this sort was to be successful, it had to have visual materials.

E. CHURCH PUBLICATIONS

130. Interfaith Center on Corporate Responsibility.
"Formula for Malnutrition." *CIC Brief* NY: ICCR, April 1975.
This *Brief* contains the substantive text of the narration to the controversial film by the same name that was also issued during this time. The tone is very hostile towards formula feeding, frequently interchanging the terms "bottle feeding" and "formula feeding".

131. Interfaith Center on Corporate Responsibility.
   "Leaders Guide for Using 'Bottle Babies'." NY: ICCR, June 1977.
   Various groups which were promoting the Nestle boycott helped to
   distribute the film "Bottle Babies". This leaders' guide which accompanied the film calls the film a "subjective, emotional, unequivocal
   . . . polemic against the manufacturers of infant formula". The leaders'
   guide attributes the efforts of infant formula companies in less-
   developed countries to declining markets in the West. The guide also
   condemns what it calls aggressive advertising techniques, and suggests certain things to say before showing the film and explains how
   one might conduct a discussion afterward.

132. Margulies, Leah.
   "Baby Formula Abroad: Exporting Infant Malnutrition." *Christianity and
   Crisis* 35(18):264, November 10, 1975.
   The thesis of this article is that products from the developed world are
   being inappropriately sold into Third World economies in which the
   products become positively dangerous. In addition, the need for corporate profits drives businesses to market their products globally.
   Infant formula is just one example of the corporate drive for profits,
   even if the effects are harmful.

133. World Council of Churches.
   Programme Unit on Justice and Service.
   "Report of the Geneva Consultation of a Proposed Action/Reflection Programme
   on Transnational Corporations, June 13-18, 1977."
   Although having nothing directly to do with the Nestle boycott, this
   proposal provides a clearer understanding of the modern church and
   church organizations' commitment to economic reorganization along
   lines described as more just and participatory.

F. INFANT FOOD INDUSTRY PUBLICATIONS

134. Abbott/Ross Laboratories.
   "Code of Marketing Ethics for Developing Countries with Reference to Infant
   Feeding, Revised." Chicago: Abbott Laboratories, Winter 1977.
   In this three page statement one U.S. company sets out its own
   marketing code in which it emphasizes the importance of breastfeeding
   for the first four to six months. It also presents its decision not to mass
   market formula but, instead, to rely upon the health care professionals
   in various countries to advise for or against the use of formula. Also
   included is its instruction to its own representatives in less-developed
   countries not to engage in deceptive or unethical practices.

135. Abbott/Ross Laboratories.
   "Notice to Distributors and Retailers of Infant Formula Regarding Your Role in
   the Delivery of Health Care Products." Chicago: Abbott Laboratories, 1977.
   This directive to distributors and retailers of infant formula for Abbott
   Laboratories states in simple language that sellers have the responsibility to determine if families requesting formula can afford it and to
   see to it that they are instructed in the proper preparation of formula

so that the formula itself does not become dangerous to the children consuming it.

136. Abbott/Ross Laboratories.
"Notice to Health Professionals." Chicago: Abbott Laboratories, c. 1978. By this notice to health professionals who may have been recommending the use of Abbott's infant formula Similac, Abbott alerts the recipients that the use of artificial feeds is usually more costly than breastfeeding. In such situations parents may be tempted to dilute the mixture to make it go farther. The health professional is told to warn against over-dilution. Secondly, the notice stresses the need for the health professional to give proper instructions to parents on the sanitary preparation of formula, especially where water may be contaminated and refrigeration is not generally available.

137. Adeniyi, Adeoye.
"The Place of Artificial Feeding in Africa." Statement, IDR (I)-26-GB. Available from Nestle Coordination Center on Nutrition, Inc., Washington, D.C. Dr. Adeniyi presents arguments in favor of artificial formula feeding in cases when mothers die or are sick, when mothers fail to produce sufficient milk, or when the child has reached three months of age and begins to need supplemental feeding. Adeniyi's presentation is worth reading because it is made by a pediatric physician working out of a Nigerian hospital with first-hand knowledge of the maladies which afflict children in the less-developed countries. The statement adds yet another dimension to the complex formula feeding dispute.

138. Ballabriga, A., H. Hilpert and H. Isliker.
"Immunity of the Infantile Gastrointestinal Tract and Implications on Modern Infant Feeding." *Nestle Research News* (24), 1974-1975. This article explains the results of therapeutic trials in which hyperimmune bovine colostral immunoglobulins, were given orally to infants suffering from infectious diarrhea. The results show a significant effect both in experimental animals and in newborn infants.

139. Bauer, E. Steven.
"Marketing Infant Foods." *Lancet* July 2, 1977. Writing on behalf of ICIFI, Bauer argues that the ICIFI Code is an important first step in self-regulation. He states that the comparison of the ICIFI Code with a similar code published by the Swedish Pediatrics Association is not justified since the two codes are meant to deal with different societies and different marketing problems.

140. Furer, A.
"Nestle and Infant Feeding in the Third World." Mimeo. Vevey, Switzerland: *Nestle,* November 18, 1975. This statement notes that the company has instituted legal action against those who published "Nestle Kills Babies", that is, the Third World Working Group.

141. International Council of Infant Food Industries.
Annual Report. ICIFI, November 1975 to September 1976. ICIFI, The International Council of Infant Food Industries, was

formed in 1975 by Nestle and seven other major manufacturers. Founding members first adopted a "Code of Ethics and Professional Standards" for advertising and promotion of breast milk substitutes. This first annual report refers to that activity and to general organizational matters. The forming of ICIFI marked the first formal cooperation among major formula companies. The industry group was formed well before the initiation of the boycott.

142. International Council of Infant Food Industries.
"Code of Ethics and Professional Standards for Advertising, Product Information and Advisory Services for Breast-Milk Substitutes." 1977.
This is a thirteen section code dated September 1976 and copyrighted by ICIFI, 1977, being a "code of ethics and professional standards for advertising, product information and advisory services for breast-milk substitutes." Although ICIFI adopted the code, it was criticized by activist groups as being ambiguous. Nevertheless, the adoption showed a willingness to consider self-regulation as a way to change certain practices.

143. International Council of Infant Food Industries.
"Infant Feeding in the Less Developed Countries: An Industry Viewpoint." *PAG Bulletin* 7, Nos. 3 and 4:62, 1977.
This infant food industry statement contains a brief discussion of the aims of ICIFI, a helpful categorization of the users of infant formula in the less-developed world, and a presentation of views and evidence on subjects such as whether lactation in a given mother is adequate, whether there has been an actual decline in breastfeeding, the cost of infant formula, and the central issue of the relationship between early supplementation and infectious diseases. The issues are well-documented, and the statement contains a list of forty-three useful and important references.

144. International Council of Infant Food Industries.
"International Council of Infant Food Industries: A Review of Its Objectives and Activities." ICIFI, September 1977.
ICIFI issued this pamphlet on its composition and activities. Contained in the publication are objectives, a list of members and a short history of ICIFI.

145. Mauron, J. and H. R. Muller.
"The Problem of Malnutrition," and "Nutrition and Infant Mortality." Berne, Switzerland: Nestle, 1976.
These two pieces published together by Nestle present the work of Nestle scientists on the subject of infant feeding and formula use. In the first article, the writer argues that to make infant formula the culprit for malnutrition is to distort the facts. The article stresses the use of formula for supplementation. The second article has as its thesis that infant mortality is falling everywhere including the developing world. The charts and graphs provided are most helpful. Low birth weight is also discussed as an important determinant of infant survival. Since supplementation is so important, control of formula by regulation may do real harm to the health of infants in less-developed countries. A rather long list of references is attached.

146. Muller, H. R.
"Infant Nutrition Today: A New Rationale in Infant Feeding?" *Nestle Research News* 12:3, 1974-1975.

Inadequate maternal nutrition and frequently recurring pregnancies are the main factors leading to a high incidence of low-birth-weight infants in developing countries. In such cases, 40% in figures which the author cites, breastfeeding is often impossible and in other cases, not advisable. Even where breastfeeding is feasible, the article argues that there is a need for supplementation of the breast milk at no later than five months. The article refers to the generally declining infant mortality rates in developing countries, and says that breastfeeding is the best choice for early months of infancy because breast milk contains essential food elements and avoids risks of contamination. Muller then discusses the physiological maturation of infants and the different calorie and protein needs at various stages of growth. He explains the components of humanized milk formula which modern food processors have developed.

147. Nestle.
Annual Reports: The Group's Activities, Nestle S.A., Unilac, Inc. Switzerland: Nestle S.A., 1977.

This annual report contains useful information to the student of the formula controversy such as net profits as a percentage of sales (to Europeans, percentage of turnover) which for 1977 was 4.1%, a chart of net profits of various product groups, new product developments, balance sheet and profit and loss statement, and abundant photographs of products and plants throughout the world.

148. Nestle.
"Infant Feeding in the Developing Countries." Nestle Products Technical Assistance Co. Ltd., Switzerland, edited by the Infant and Dietetic Products Dept., 1977.

There is ample pictorial presentation of Nestle ads in this publication put out by Nestle itself. Radio spots and their content are referred to and field workers are pictured as well. Of course, all of this is prior to the complete discontinuance by Nestle of this kind of activity. Also included is a discussion of Nestle's view of itself as it sells in less-developed countries.

149. Nestle.
"Infant Nutrition in the Developing Countries . . . . What Others Think About It." Nestle IDR (I)-27-GB, c. 1977.

This is a series of quotations from various sources about Nestle's sale and promotion of infant formula. Some of the statements are general, while others refer specifically to the charges, made by the Third World Working Group, that Nestle was responsible for the deaths of thousands of infants in less-developed countries.

150. Nestle.
"Libel Proceedings: Nestle Alimentana S.A. Against 'Arbeitsgruppe Dritte Welt'." Berne, Switzerland: Nestle, June 1976.

This document is the Nestle "documentation for the press" provided as part of the libel trial against the Third World Working Group in Berne, Switzerland during June of 1976.

151. Nestle.
Nestle in the Developing Countries. Vevey, Switzerland: Nestle Alimentana
S.A., 1975.
This 228-page book on the development of the sale of Nestle products
in South and Central America, Asia, and Africa is amply illustrated
by pictures and graphs. The date of Nestle's entry into the economy of
a particular country is given along with a brief discussion of the types
of products sold in each area. Although produced by Nestle itself, the
account shows the diverse and complex ways in which the worldwide
food company provides goods to remote areas of the globe. Researchers
would want to read this account as a means of better understanding
the view of the company to its socio-economic contributions worldwide.

152. Nestle.
"The Story Behind the Issue: Infant Feeding in Developing Countries."
Washington, D.C.: Nestle Coordination Center for Nutrition, undated.
In a question/answer format this pamphlet asks and states answers
to certain questions which have pervaded the Nestle controversy. Has
infant mortality increased? Have promotional activities of formula
companies led to a decline in breastfeeding? Is Nestle doing anything
to ensure that its products are being safely used? The answers are
challenging and thought-provoking.

III. THE BOYCOTT PHASE — EXPANSION OF THE POPULAR
CAMPAIGN: 1978-1981

A. GENERAL ARTICLES AND STUDIES

153. Aberbach, Pauline, et al.
"Nestle and the Infant Formula Controversy." *Yale School of Organization
and Management,* c. 1979.
The timing of this case study prevented its recognition of promotional
policy changes instituted by Nestle. On some issues the presentation
is balanced; on others, anti-industry sources are largely used. Conclu-
sory language, such as describing Nestle practices as "questionable"
without explaining the reasons for the conclusion, seems inappropriate
to a case study.

154. Abrams, Elliott.
"Discussion of the WHO Code on Infant Formula." Address by Elliott Abrams,
Assistant Secretary of State for International Organization Affairs, Sponsored
by The Heritage Foundation, Washington, D.C., June 19, 1981.
In this speech defending the vote of the United States against the
adoption of the World Health Organization's International Code of
Marketing of Breastmilk Substitutes, Abrams summarizes the basic
issues in the controversy and asserts that much of the public debate
has its origins in political and economic views which generally oppose
Western profit-making corporations. The speech discloses the reasons
for the United States' controversial vote on the Code.

155. Abrams, Elliott.
"The U.S. Position on Infant Feeding." *Nutrition Today* p. 12, July/August 1981.
The Assistant Secretary of State briefly clarifies the reasons for the U.S. government's position against the WHO Code of Marketing of Breastmilk Substitutes.

156. Adelman, Carol.
"Infant Formula Marketing Code." Memorandum to Elliott Abrams, Assistant Secretary, Department of State, Washington, D.C., April 8, 1981.
This informative memorandum highlights the deliberations of U.S. government officials as they considered what the U.S. position should be on the WHO International Code of Marketing of Breastmilk Substitutes and related issues. The memo discusses the major assumptions of the proponents of the Code and subjects those assumptions to scientific and logical scrutiny. The memo does not oppose the idea of a code of marketing, but it does point out that an overly restrictive code may actually keep formula from being available to those who need it and who could properly use it.

157. Administrative Committee on Co-ordination.
"Dietary Management of Young Infants Who Are Not Adequately Breast Fed." *U.N. University Food and Nutrition Bulletin* 2:41, 1980.
This publication is in the form of guidelines directed to health-care workers who encounter infants in the early months of their lives who are not being breastfed or who are being breastfed, but not receiving adequate nourishment. The health workers who were able to convey the helpful suggestions and instructions contained in this publication could do much to reduce the hazards of improper preparation and use of formula and other non-commercial breastmilk substitutes.

158. Ahn, Chung Hae and William C. MacLean.
"Growth of the Exclusively Breast-Fed Infant." *American Journal of Clinical Nutrition* 33:183, February 1980.
This United States' study was made of 96 infants whose mothers breastfed them exclusively for at least the first six months, with the average duration of breastfeeding being seven months. The mothers were all members of the La Leche League International, and therefore proponents of breastfeeding. The weight and length curves of the infants studied remained above the 50th percentile on the National Center for Health Statistics population for at least the sixth month of life. The applicability of these findings to less-developed countries is suggested, but with the understanding that the mothers' diets would have to be supplemented in most parts of the less-developed world.

159. Almroth, S., T. Greiner and M. C. Latham.
"Economic Importance of Breastfeeding." *Food and Nutrition* 5(2):5, 1979.
The authors attempt to place a U.S. dollar value on the cost of formula feeding an infant under certain assumed circumstances as opposed to breastfeeding the same child. The authors use data from Ghana and the Ivory Coast while making assumptions about how long the child would be fed exclusively with formula and how long with mixed feeding. The savings for the nation, if one accepts all the authors'

assumptions, is between 16 and 20 million U.S. dollars. Certain cross checks used by the authors show that this estimate may be too high. Other benefits of breastfeeding, such as child spacing, are said to be unmeasurable.

160. American Academy of Pediatrics.
"Breast-Feeding." *Journal of Pediatrics* 2:591, 1978.
This article reiterates certain information for the physician who is advising mothers about infant feeding. Statistics from Canada and the United States show an initial decline of breastfeeding in both countries in the post World War II era, but followed by a partial resurgence of interest in it. Factors responsible for the decline of breastfeeding are discussed.

161. Anthony, Catherine M.
"Boycott." *Visitor* p. 3, June 22, 1980.
The author explains the main issues in the controversy in a well-balanced presentation. The INFACT demands get comparatively more space that the industry responses but Anthony offers some rebuttal to her readers.

162. Apple, Rima D.
"To Be Used Only Under the Direction of a Physician: Commercial Infant Feeding and Medical Practice 1870-1940." *Bulletin of the History of Medicine* 54(3):402, Fall 1980.
The writer argues that, beginning in the 1870s and moving forward to the 1930s, infant food companies in this country gradually enlisted the medical profession on their behalf. Physicians saw that physician control and advice about the use of artificial baby feeds were important to proper use. By the end of the period studied, the infant formula companies had established a mutually advantageous relationship with the medical community. The article contains some interesting material on the development of infant formula and feeds in the United States.

163. Baer, Edward and Leah Margulies.
"Infant and Young Child Feeding: An Analysis of the WHO/UNICEF Meeting." *Studies in Family Planning* 11(2):72, February 1980.
This short report on the proceedings of the WHO/UNICEF meeting held in October 1979 in Geneva on the subject of infant formula feeding is written by two persons who have been supporters of the Nestle boycott. They point out that for the first time in United Nations' history, certain activist groups were allowed to participate under the designation "NGO" (non-governmental organizations). The report also presents a "behind the scenes" look, from the viewpoint of the activist groups, of the strategy and maneuvering of Nestle and other industry people to achieve a result that would be as unrestrictive as possible.

164. Baer, Edward and Leah Margulies.
"An Intriguing Delivery." *Development Forum* July/August 1981.
This article accuses Nestle and the infant formula industry of using "dirty tricks" to prevent the passage of the WHO Code. In addition, the authors trace the controversy as it led up to the 1981 enactment of

the Code. The article repeats the theme that infant formula companies constantly try to influence, pressure and coerce physicians, researchers, governments and others to adopt their position. Baer and Margulies have taken a consistently critical stance toward formula feeding, and it is well illustrated by this presentation.

165. Ball, R.
"Nestle Revs Up Its U.S. Campaign." *Fortune* 97:80, February 13, 1978. This article is a recent piece on the history of Nestle S.A. Considerable mention is made of Arthur Furer, then President and Chief Executive of Nestle, as well as insights into the company's philosophy of management. The formula feeding dispute is only briefly mentioned. This is good background material of Nestle from a business magazine's viewpoint.

166. Beatty, Sharon.
"Infant Formula: A Nutritional Nightmare." *Peace Corps Times* 3:3, July/August 1980.
The author takes a level look at the controversy and is critical of both sides. While identifying the boycott with "the stuff of slogans", such as "capitalists exploiting the masses", Ms. Beatty argues that most infant diarrhea is bottle induced, and that traditional weaning foods are excellent, at least in Yemen. She concludes that emphasis and effort should be directed towards educating Third World people in nutrition rather than an emotional boycott.

167. Bellini, James.
"Behind the Closed Doors of Nestlegate." *Vision,* May 1981.
This article maintains that Nestle S.A., which the author calls "the men of Vevey", produced a product which scored failing grades like no other product in the history of marketing. The writer portrays Nestle S.A. as channeling money to third parties who would oppose the boycott of Nestle products and as wanting to maintain their "grip" on the marketing of products to the less-developed world. The thrust and tone of the article are anti-infant formula industry.

168. "The Bottle Battle: A Third World Problem."
Bostonia (Boston University Alumni Magazine), Fall 1978.
This article is openly hostile towards Nestle, and relies more on jargon and cliché than on facts and analysis.

169. Bradshaw, Thornton and David Vogel.
"Business and the Political Environment: Ethical Questions." In: Corporations and Their Critics: Issues and Answers to the Problems of Corporate Social Responsibility. New York: McGraw-Hill Book Company, 1981; p. 80.
The response of Nestle to early criticisms is cited by the writers of this work. The authors agree that Nestle at first went on the offensive, referring to the libel suit, but then shifted to a more positive position of engaging in dialogue with its critics.

170. Buchan, Jane.
"The 'Bottle Baby' Syndrome." *International Nursing Review* 26 (5):141, September/October 1979.
The writer is a nurse who is convinced that bottle feeding is the

primary cause of malnutrition and disease in less-developed countries. She refers to the problem as the "bottle baby syndrome". She asserts that a trend toward bottle feeding has developed and in most cases the shift from breastfeeding has not been necessary because of the mother's inability to physically produce milk but because of urbanization, promotion of bottle feeding and status consciousness. These conclusions are not documented by references. The writer suggests that the nursing profession should support legislation which would ban the advertising of formula feeding under certain circumstances.

171. Bullough, Vern L.
"Bottle Feeding: An Amplification." *Bulletin of the History of Medicine* 55(2):257, Summer 1981.
The author explains the history of the rubber nipple beginning with its "invention" in 1845 and its development in the 1860s and 1870s. He also cites some instances of wet nursing and pap feeding in earlier periods.

172. Butz, William P.
"Economic Aspects of Breastfeeding." In: Mosely, W. H., ed. Nutrition and Human Reproduction. New York: Plenum Press, 1978; p. 231.
The author uses an opportunity-cost approach to the mother's choice to breastfeed pointing out that breastfeeding uses the mother's time and energy which could be used in another way. Butz argues that in terms of total benefits and costs to the family of the mother of the newborn, greater efforts should be devoted to overcoming the undesirable effects of less breastfeeding rather than attempting to reverse what may be a perfectly defensible shift away from breastfeeding in an urban industrialized culture.

173. Canadian Pediatric Society.
"Breastfeeding: What Is Left Besides the Poetry?" *Canadian Journal of Public Health* 69:13, 1978.
The writers of this article review the benefits of breast milk, nutritionally and immunologically. In addition, they offer various suggestions for increasing the acceptance of breastfeeding once again, especially during the first three to six months of the infant's life.

174. Chandra, R. K.
"Immunological Aspects of Human Milk." *Nutrition Review* 36:265, 1978.
The unique qualities of human milk, including, but not limited to, its protein make-up, antibodies, and other infection-resisting components, make it responsible for the decreased incidence of infections and other respiratory and gastrointestinal disorders when the infant consumes it rather than substitutes.

175. Clarkson, Fred.
"Growing Nestle Boycott Haunts Infant Formula Makers." *Womens International Network News* p. 12, March 1, 1981.
This piece makes the often repeated argument of the INFACT group that formula sales practices are responsible for thousands of deaths and millions of malnourished infants in the Third World.

176. Cole, Elizabeth.
"Breast-Feeding: A Critique of the Literature." In: Raphael, Dana, ed. Breast-feeding and Food Policy in a Hungry World. New York: Academic Press, 1978.
This chapter in Raphael's book has considerable significance because researcher Cole reports a number of serious flaws in published studies on comparative effects of breastfeeding and artificial feeding, including unreliable sampling techniques. She reviewed 350 studies.

177. Constable, Elinor.
"Statement of Ms. Elinor Constable, Deputy Assistant Secretary of State for International Finance and Development, Bureau of Economic and Business Affairs before the Subcommittee on International Economic Policy and Trade of the House Foreign Affairs Committee, June 16, 1981." Department of State: Washington, D.C., 1981.
These remarks are made in defense of the Reagan administration's decision not to support the WHO Code.

178. Crain, Lance.
"Interview with Pierre Liotard-Vogt." *Advertising Age* p. 31, June 30, 1980.
This is a general discussion of Nestle chief, Pierre Liotard-Vogt's, view of Nestle and some of the effects of the boycott on the international food products firm.

179. Davies, D. P.
"Is Inadequate Breastfeeding an Important Cause of Failure to Thrive?" *Lancet* i:541, 1979.
This piece points out that breastfeeding, especially by mothers who are breastfeeding for the first time, can result in underfeeding. Inadequate lactation was diagnosed in 9 out of 21 infants admitted to an English maternity hospital. The author stresses the need for proper instruction in the practical process of breastfeeding.

180. Dawson, K. P., et al.
"Keeping Abreast of the Times: The Tauraunga Infant Feeding Survey." *New Zealand Medical Journal* 89:75, 1979.
This study is based upon the feeding habits of mothers located in the town of Tauraunga on the North Island of New Zealand. The dates covered are 1976 to early 1977. Predictably, the mothers gradually abandoned breastfeeding following their discharge from the hospital. Over 77% breastfed upon discharge, but that percentage had fallen to slightly over 56% at the end of three months. The most commonly given reason for the discontinuance of breastfeeding was insufficient milk.

181. Epstein, Edwin M. and Lee E. Preston, eds.
"The Infant Formula Issue: A Case Study." Business Environment/Public Policy: The Field and Its Future. Proceedings of the AACSB Summer Conference, St. Louis, MO: American Assembly of Collegiate Schools of Business, 1981.
This case study is composed of two statements, one by David Cox of Ross Laboratories and the other by Mary Gardner Jones of Western Union Telegraph Company. Cox outlines the numerous factors which affect the business enterprise, especially in the Third World, including population, literacy, education, mobility, mortality, water supplies,

and the like. In this context he discusses the use of infant formula as a substitute for breast milk. Jones discusses the ethical questions raised about business practices in the context Cox has set.

182. Family Life Foundation.
"Infant Formula in the Third World: Does It Serve a Useful Role?" Washington, D.C.: Family Life Foundation, May 9, 1979.
This booklet contains the presentations by and questioning of participants in a conference conducted in May of 1979. Participants obviously hold different viewpoints on the issue of formula feeding. All are physicians or health professionals and most have had first-hand experience in Third World countries. The presentations serve to caution those who are convinced that surveys from Third World mothers on the subject of feeding are reliable.

183. Fildes, Valerie.
"On the Bottle Again." *Nursing Mirror* 151(5):31, December 11, 1980.
The author maintains that weaning practices from 1660 to 1880 often contributed to the sickness and death of infants. The evidence is derived from various sources including diaries, writers' comments and autobiographies. Sometimes infant mortality was attributed to teething, but the writer believes that since teething and weaning foods often came together, the introduction of weaning was often overlooked as the true cause of disease and difficulty. Some of the conclusions are speculative given the scanty evidence.

184. Fomon, S. J. and R. G. Strauss.
"Nutrient Deficiencies in Breast-Fed Infants." *New England Journal of Medicine* 299:355, 1978.
Normal, healthy, full-term infants, breastfed by healthy mothers, may still develop deficiencies of iron and vitamin D, in which cases supplementation is desirable. In addition, thiamin and B_{12} deficiencies may develop in infants who are breastfed by mothers who themselves are nutritionally deficient.

185. Gelardi, Robert C.
"The Infant Formula Issue: A Story in Simplification and Escalation." *Nutrition Today* p. 26, September/October 1981.
This document helps the reader to appreciate the development of the formula controversy, noting how it began and what the current state of knowledge is on the problem. It suggests that public and private groups work together to solve the remaining problems. A specific list of the known facts at the time the essay was written is provided.

186. Gerlach, L. P.
"Flea and the Elephant: Infant Formula Controversy." *Society* 17:51 September/October 1980.
In this article, appearing in the peak year of the controversy, anthropologist Gerlach steps back from the particulars of the Nestle controversy to analyze the dynamics of the dispute. He points out that it is hard to research the issue because of the ideological convictions of the protest groups and the complexity of the questions presented. In addition, industry public relations efforts and legitimate endeavors to make itself more socially responsive add to the problem of sorting out

truth from partial truth. The narrower issues are part of a larger attempt to reorient business to the interests of certain consumerist groups and to compel business to pay attention to the social goals which various church groups deem important.

187. Gladwin, Thomas N. and Ingo Walter.
"The Infant Formula Controversy." In: Multinationals Under Fire: Lessons in the Management of Conflict. New York: John Wiley & Sons, 1980; p. 361.
Chapter 10 of this book deals with the problems of marketing that multinational companies face. Approximately ten pages are devoted to the Nestle controversy as a short example case. The presentation ends with October 1979. Much of the material presented is footnoted to sources which opposed Nestle, such as INFACT and others. Reference is made to other similar marketing controversies and also to a host of other problems which multinational companies face when they sell products into the less-developed world.

188. Goldsmith, Clifford, ed.
"Multinationals and Health, Part I." *Critical Health* 2:5, 1980.
This article purports to demonstrate that milk supplements are harmful to infants.

189. Goodwin, Shirley.
"The Baby-milk Controversy: When Milk Doesn't Come First." *Nursing Mirror* 152(5):31, January 29, 1981.
The writer is a nurse who warns other nurses to be aware of the hidden effects which promotional efforts of formula companies may have on their professional judgment. She believes that posters, pens, visits by company representatives and booklets do have the effect of biasing the advice of health workers and midwives in favor of one product over another. The article then discusses the Nestle controversy, although there is reference to other infant food companies as well. She calls upon health centers and nurses to be aware of the unwitting support that may be given to a product or mode of feeding by the mere presence of posters and the like in hospital settings.

190. Gueri, Miguel.
"Some Economic Implications of Breastfeeding." *Cajanus* 13:85, 1980.
According to the calculations of this article, feeding an infant with formula would cost 4 to 5 times what it would cost to supplement a mother during lactation in order to stimulate an adequate supply of breast milk. The figures are based upon experience in Trinidad. Assuming that both formula and maternal supplements had to be imported, the amount of foreign exchange would be much higher for the formula approach than for the maternal supplement approach.

191. Hakim, Peter.
"Programs to Encourage Breastfeeding in the Developing Countries." In: Raphael, D., ed. Breastfeeding and Food Policy in a Hungry World, New York: Academic Press, 1978.
This section in Raphael's book discusses the problems connected with attempts to get more women to continue breastfeeding in the face of a tendency for them to use formula in a bottle.

192. Harrison, Neil.
"Nestle Alimentana S.A. — Infant Formula: A Case Study." Harvard Business School, 1980.
This 13-page Harvard Business School case study largely devotes itself to the economics of the formula controversy.

193. Hartwick, Nanci.
"Infant Formula: A Threat to Third-World Babies." *Graduate Woman* p. 26, November/December 1981.
Ms. Hartwick claims that firms exploit Third World mothers by convincing them to bottle feed instead of breastfeed. This represents a rehearsal of the standard view found in INFACT materials. The reference to Nestle's position is limited to an unnamed Nestle official's statement.

194. Herbert, Pearl.
"Putting A Case for the Breast." *Nursing Mirror* 149(3):1921, July 19, 1979.
The reasons for preferring breastfeeding to infant formula feeding are well presented by this short article. Herbert argues that breast milk is easier to digest, makes the baby more resistant to infection, and may act as a contraceptive. The author says that the choice remains with the parents after careful consideration, but the author believes that the case for breastfeeding is very strong.

195. Hickel, James.
"Infant Formula: WHO Mixes It Up." *Reason* p. 41, December 1981.
This eight-page essay criticizes the arguments of Nestle's opponents, focusing on factual errors and anecdotal reasoning.

196. Hicks, Guy M.
"The Infant Formula Controversy." *The Backgrounder* No. 142, Washington, D.C.: The Heritage Foundation, May 14, 1981.
This paper summarizes the facts of the controversy up to the time of the passage of the WHO Code in May 1981.

197. Human Lactation Center.
"Mixed Feeding Keeps Babies Alive." *The Lactation Review* 3:1, 1978.
One of the findings of the Human Lactation Center is that in the less-developed world infant mortality has decreased in the three decades prior to 1973 when food prices began to go up. Breast milk is the best form of infant food but breast milk alone is not adequate as the exclusive source of nutrition past the third month. Mixed feeding is the usual pattern in less-developed countries. The assumption that breastfeeding worldwide is on the decline has not been verified.

198. "Infant Formula: An Activist Campaign."
Europe's Consumer Movement: Key Issues and Corporate Responses. Geneva, Switzerland: Business International, S.A., 1980.
Excerpted from a longer report on the consumer movement in Europe, this chapter is a dispassionate analysis of the formula feeding dispute through 1980. The main scientific issues are discussed as well as the composition of the activist groups. There is a helpful, brief treatment of the obtaining of "NGO" (non-governmental organization) status

under United Nations' rules by the opponents of Nestle. The advantages and disadvantages of dealing with international deliberative bodies also comes through.

199. Jackson, John H.
"Transnational Enterprises and International Codes of Conduct: Introductory Remarks for Experts." *Law Quadrangle Notes* (University of Michigan Law School, Ann Arbor, Michigan) 25 (2):18, Winter, 1981.
World environmental interdependence and the vital role played by transnational enterprises are the subjects of this brief article. The author examines the benefits and dangers of these large business enterprises and the need for careful, enforceable yet flexible codes of conduct and ethics. The article is useful in illuminating some of the problems faced on both sides of the issue and has practical applicability to the exchanges between infant formula proponents and those favoring adoption of the WHO Code.

200. Jelliffe, E. F. P.
"The Impact of the Food Industry on the Nutritional Status of Young Children in Developing Countries." In: Mayer, J. and J. Dwyer, eds. Food and Nutrition Policy in a Changing World. New York: Oxford University Press, 1979; p. 197.
The author suggests certain problems with artificial feeding in less-developed countries. These are incorrect dilution of formula and inadequate sterilizaton of utensils used in the preparation. Also mentioned is the high cost of formula feeding contrasted with the low incomes of those living in less-developed countries. Factors such as general poverty, poor education and generally poor sanitation all contribute to the above mentioned problems.

201. Kimberling, Sidney R.
"Supporting Breast-Feeding." *Pediatrics* 63:60, January 1979.
The author, a physician with considerable experience in counseling breastfeeding, explains the need for instilling confidence in the nursing mother who is often subject to easy discouragement due to lack of support, inadequate knowledge of breastfeeding techniques and fatigue. The article contains a useful summary of "hints" about breastfeeding and suggested readings for the consulting physician.

202. King, Christine and Eloise Clawson.
"Infant Feeding in Developing Nations." *The Massachusetts Nurse* 49(5):5, May 1980.
Two nurses review in a popular presentation the formula feeding controversy and then urge other nurses to write to Nestle, support legislation against formula sales abroad and join in the Nestle boycott. This is an example of how convictions were translated into action.

203. Kunt, Aylin.
"Nestle and the Infant Food Controversy." *IMEDE,* School of Business Administration, London, Ontario, Canada, 1981.
The Nestle controversy became the subject of numerous case studies. This is one intended for use in management classes. The case contains materials provided by Nestle and by activist groups opposing Nestle. The scientific evidence is not particularly well presented. Some of the

tangential disputes, for example, the materials dealing with Professor Bwibo's view of the "Bottle Babies" film and the inclusion of the attacks on Nestle for their support of the Ethics and Public Policy Center, receive too much attention. They do, however, show the magnitude of the distrust and the possibility of misunderstandings when popular presentations simplify complicated realities.

204. Manoff, R. K. and T. M. Cooke.
"Whose Milk Shall We Market?" *Journal of Tropical Pediatrics* 26:ii, 1980.
If health professionals wish to promote breastfeeding, they can borrow the techniques of commercial marketing. The messages should be carefully designed to appeal to the desired group and then tested to determine audience response.

205. Marchione, T. J.
"A History of Breastfeeding Practices in the English-speaking Caribbean in the Twentieth Century." *Food and Nutrition Bulletin* 2:9, 1980.
This historical presentation of present and past child-feeding practices in the Caribbean shows that the artificial feeding of native gruels by the third or fourth month was common in the first quarter of this century. The author says that whatever the initiating cause of artificial feeding, the food industry was not the initiator of such practices.

206. Mata, L. J.
"Breastfeeding: Main Promoter of Infant Health." *American Journal of Clinical Nutrition* 31:2058, 1978.
The advantages of breastfeeding ought to be presented to mothers before, during and after pregnancy, especially in societies which are moving from agricultural to urban. Mothers-to-be should be made aware of the need for supplementation to their own diets in order to help produce proper lactation.

207. McGinnis, James B.
Bread and Justice: Toward a New International Economic Order. Ch. 12: "Nestle: A Case Study of a Multinational Corporation."
The author devotes an entire chapter to the Nestle dispute. McGinnis' position is that Nestle is engaged in destructive marketing practices in the Third World. Nestle controls capital, redirecting it from other much needed projects to the unnecessary production of a "convenience food". Nestle, according to the author, also inappropriately uses technology to sell and produce its formula, as well as imposing its products upon consumers by mass marketing techniques. This "case study" is a one-sided attack on formula feeding and Nestle. Quotations are almost uniformly from Nestle's most outspoken critics. The case study ends with a call similar to INFACT pamphlets for the reader to join the boycott and to encourage others to do so.

208. McPherson, M. P. and Elliott Abrams.
"Infant Formula Code." *Department State Bulletin* 81:54, July 1981.
Statements by Abrams and McPherson explain the care that was taken by the United States government as it considered whether it could or could not vote in favor of the WHO Code which would serve as a model for regulating infant formula feeding worldwide. The reasons

given by the government of the United States were that the Code posed serious legal and constitutional problems, that the Code did not allow sufficient nation-by-nation flexibility to make adjustments in its provisions due to legal, social, or economic conditions and that the Code, were it to be applied in the United States, would have been an unwarranted invasion of the freedom of men and women to make informed choices.

209. Murray, J. Alex, ed.
Food Processing in North America: A Struggle for Survival. Windsor, Ontario: Institute for Canadian-American Studies, November 13, 1981.
These proceedings, the result of the 23rd Annual Seminar conducted by the Institute, contain one article of importance for understanding the Nestle controversy. The article on the subject of corporate responsibility used the Nestle dispute as an example of the volatility of an issue in today's world of fast-paced communications and action groups. John A. Sparks, of Public Policy Education Fund, Inc., who has written articles on the controversy which have been generally favorable to Nestle, takes up such questions as the use of native weaning foods, the use of commercial feeds, the promotion practices of Nestle, and then points out that issues like those raised by the controversy can be enduring issues if they can attract support from diverse action organizations. Readers are reminded that Nestle had arrayed against it breastfeeding groups, women's rights groups, natural foods groups, socially active churches, consumerists, and radical leftist groups. The piece also notes that the reputations of large firms are exceedingly fragile.

210. Murray, J. Alex.
"Nestle in LDCs." University of Windsor: International Business Studies Unit, 1981.
This is a case study of the Nestle formula feeding controversy. Murray includes information and documents from various groups which became involved in the public debate. Unfortunately the case was created in 1981 so that the developments of the resolution of the controversy are not included.

211. Nickel, Herman.
"Corporation Haters." *Fortune* 101:126, June 16, 1980.
This article refers frequently to the Nestle controversy. Nickel's main purpose, however, seems to be to point out to American business that a coalition of leftist and some church-affiliated groups are intent upon opposing multinational corporations whenever there is an opportunity. Nickel gives examples to illustrate his contention that many sincere and well-meaning church people add credibility to those groups which are the hard-core opponents of free enterprise economies. There is no new information in this article but, instead, the reorganization of material to advance Nickel's theses.

212. Pinckney, Carol R.
"Third World Women and Children Need More Than a Boycott!" *Journal of Nurse-Midwifery* 25:25, May/June 1980.
The author blames poverty and its many ramifications for the plight

of Third World children. The formula industry has been much less to "blame" for the morbidity/mortality of poor infants. Supplements are much needed and efforts to discourage the availability of proper supplements will not help the children concerned.

213. Pinckney, Carol R.
"The Baby Bottle Controversy: A Rejoinder." *Journal of Nurse-Midwifery* 26(2):32, March/April 1981.
The writer's thesis is that breastfeeding, though desirable for various reasons, will not solve the problems of infant health in the Third World because they are caused by a multiplicity of factors including fetal and maternal malnutrition, endemic disease, unsanitary environment, protein/calorie scarcity and others. The author insists upon care in properly identifying the problem, putting the problem in a proper context and facilitating understanding as opposed to championing one's cause.

214. Post, James E.
"Comparative Responses: The International Infant Formula Industry." In: Corporate Behavior and Social Change. Reston, VA: Reston Publishing Co., Inc., 1978; p. 257.
Post discusses the approaches of various infant formula companies to the challenges which were made to the marketing of infant formula in the less-developed countries. He describes Nestle as at first taking a hard line approach but later adopting a sharing approach in which it cooperated with groups in order to get their input and to make a corporate response. There is no doubt that Nestle did interact with critics and did not ignore them. Whether this represented a change from their position in the earlier part of the controversy or whether Nestle's critics produced better objections later in the dispute, remains in question.

215. Raphael, Dana.
"The Politics of Breastfeeding." *American Academy of Pediatrics* p. 14, December 1981.
The writer, a noted anthropologist, sees the WHO Code as overlooking the intricate task of women today which is to adapt to the new urban culture and, in many cases, to work and to raise young children alone. Women who are caught in a culture of poverty, evidence shows, breastfeed as long as they can. The Code puts no trust or confidence in the decision-making power or judgment of these women. The author cites the prohibition of baby bottles in New Guinea a few years ago and shows how that prohibition has led to dangerous make-shift feeding and black markets in baby bottles.

216. Richardson, B. D.
"Breast Versus Bottle Feeding." *South African Medical Journal* 53(25):1010, June 17, 1978.
This letter further discusses the breastfeeding practices of urban and rural mothers in various South African communities, especially Durban. The author is concerned about the increase in bottle feeding in some locales.

217. Rozen, Leah.
"Nestle Curtails World-Wide Consumer Ads for Formula." *Advertising Age* p. 28, April 23, 1979.
This article is a progress report up to the spring of 1979 on the dispute between Nestle and INFACT, noting the call for an international conference on the problem by the World Health Organization.

218. Savane, M.A.
"Yes to Breastfeeding, But . . . How?" *Assignment Children* 49/50:81, 1980.
The author asserts that Third World governments have, in many cases, given little attention to the problems of mothers. Many countries have not ratified the International Labor Organization conventions on maternal care. When mothers' economic and social circumstances improve, this can be expected to check the decline in breastfeeding.

219. Schoonmaker, M. E.
"Here's Looking at You, Kid." *Progressive* 45:42, December 1981.
In an argument not often made by those who oppose the formula companies, this author says that among low income or illiterate people in the United States, formula can be misused. She cites individual cases of failure to dilute and other errors in use. She maintains that there is ferocious competition among American companies, not Nestle, for hospital free-sample business. All this would need additional study because the evidence presented is only anecdotal. Nevertheless, the points made deserve to be considered along with the important factors of consumer freedom and choice.

220. Schwab, M. B.
"The Rise and Fall of the Baby's Bottle." *Journal of Human Nutrition* 33(4):276, 1979.
This general piece traces the changing attitudes of modern societies toward infant feeding. The author presents material about the effects of the industrial revolution on infant feeding and notes the shift away from breastfeeding. He calls for conciliation between the various interested parties to the modern controversy over infant feeding.

221. Schwartz, Ruth B.
"The Infant Formula Fiasco: The Lack That Will Lead to a Law." *ACSH News and Views* (American Council on Science and Health) 1(5):1, September/October 1980.
Between 1978 and 1979 certain producers of infant formula, apparently in response to consumerist groups, lowered the salt content of baby formula. Some infants who depended solely on the formula for a source of sodium chloride experienced severe reactions known as metabolic alkalosis. The formula which caused the greatest difficulty was that produced by Syntex Corporation. This incident has sometimes been mentioned by opponents of artificial formula companies but has little to do with the boycott of Nestle and the breastfeeding versus formula feeding controversy.

222. Scott-Atkinson, David.
"The Nestle Caper Is a PR Nightmare." *Marketing* October 12, 1981.
This popularly written appeal to support Nestle is penned in a style

which is light yet hard-hitting on the issues. The author says that Nestle was singled out because it had attractive boycottable products and because it was big. He is convinced that products can be misused if they are sold into countries where communication is difficult. He asserts, however, that Third World mortality is on the decrease and that companies like Nestle have played an important part in that decrease. He finally counsels an all-out public relations effort by Nestle.

223. Seitz, R.
"Baby-Bottle Battle." *Far Eastern Economic Review* 113:26, July 31-August 6, 1981.
The emphasis of this article is upon the formula feeding choices of mothers in the Philippines. According to the authors, mothers there have been greatly affected by intensive and extensive advertising by various formula companies. Quoted is Professor Virginia Guzman from the University of the Philippines who favors the adoption of the WHO Code. The article speculates that a less restrictive code will be adopted by the Philippines.

224. Tainton, Edgar M.
"About the Nestle Boycott: Kicking the Bottle." *The Christian Challenge* September 1981.
In this reivew of the Nestle controversy, the writer raises a number of crucial issues. First, if all agree that breastfeeding is the best first choice for infants, and if all agree that the products themselves as furnished by the formula companies are safe and wholesome, then where is the dispute? The bulk of the differences have to do with the propriety of certain kinds of promotion. The author also says that the choice of Third World mothers on the matter of breast versus bottle is being ignored. This is a popular piece, but provocatively written.

225. Uyanga, J.
"Rural-Urban Differences in Child Care and Breastfeeding Behavior in South-eastern Nigeria." *Social Science and Medicine* 14D:23, 1980.
Using a mathematical model developed by Barry Popkin, the author is able to show that rural-urban variations in breastfeeding choices are associated with the mother's attitude toward breastfeeding, her income, education and household make-up.

226. Van Esterik, P. and Ted Greiner.
"Breastfeeding and Women's Work: Constraints and Opportunities." *Studies in Family Planning* 12:184, 1981.
The authors dispute the view that the employment needs of mothers are important in explaining the decline in breastfeeding in some urban areas of the less-developed world. The authors refer to data from more than 30 countries in which women seldom give "work" as the reason for choosing artificial feeding over breastfeeding. The authors conclude that the area needs more research.

227. Waterlow, J. C., A. Ashworth and M. Griffiths.
"Faltering Infant Growth in Less-Developed Countries." *Lancet* 2:1176, 1980.
Fourteen less-developed countries were the subjects of this study of

infant growth during the early months of life. The authors found that growth rate falters from three to four months of age and in about half of the countries as early as two to three months. The view that the second six months of infancy are the critical growth months deserves reassessment.

228. Winikoff, Beverly.
"Nutrition, Population, and Health: Some Implications for Policy." *Science* 200:895, May 26, 1978.
Policy decisions about infant health should be the result of the input of health professionals, economists, government planners and many others, according to the writer. The promotion of child survival must be seen as an intrinsic good and the powerful capability of breastfeeding to further that end should be recognized.

229. World Health Organization.
"A Guideline for the Measurement of Nutritional Impact of Supplementary Feeding Programmes Aimed at Vulnerable Groups." Geneva: WHO, 1979.
These are guidelines intended to help health services in interested countries evaluate supplemental feeding programs that are being administered to infants, preschoolers, and early elementary school children. The guidelines are practical and understandable.

230. World Health Organization.
"Community Water Supplies: Who Pays?" *WHO Chronicle* 33:70, 1979.
The lack of potable water in parts of many less-developed countries plays an important part in the formula feeding controversy. This well-balanced argument explains two possible ways in which water is viewed by governments in the less-developed countries. First, it may be regarded as a natural or free good to which all should be entitled without cost. Second, water may be viewed as the product of an industrial process and thus costly. The author explains the arguments on both sides of the question in a thorough, balanced way.

231. Zimbabwe Government, Ministry of Health.
"Baby Feeding: Behind and Towards a Health Model for Zimbabwe." Harare/ Salisbury, Zimbabwe: The Department of Nutrition, Ministry of Health, Government of Zimbabwe, 1981.
This booklet is intended by the government of Zimbabwe to encourage breastfeeding and to discourage the use of infant formula. The provisions of the WHO Code are cited at the outset. The sources used to write the book are almost entirely those which opposed the formula industry and supported the boycott. The difficulty of formula preparation, its high cost and the likelihood of infection are all stressed. When supplements are needed, the use of local soft porridges is encouraged. The booklet counsels against the use of infant formula even as a supplement. In this regard the publication does not agree with much of scientific opinion.

B. SCIENTIFIC ARTICLES AND STUDIES

232. Addy, D. P.
"Infant Feeding." *Lancet* 2(8086):421, August 19, 1978.
This letter is a short report on the instructions found on formula tins and containers by the writer in a visit to Hong Kong two or three years earlier in which he found a confusing array of instructions for the dilution and preparation of the formula depending upon the particular brand. His letter calls for standardization.

233. Aidou, J., et al.
"Bottle Feeding and the Law in Papua, New Guinea." *Lancet* (8134):155, July 21, 1979.
This is a short letter from various physicians on the faculty of medicine at the University of Papua, New Guinea. The authors say that since 1977, according to the limited data gathered, there has been a decline in the use of bottle feeding in that country and an increase in breast-feeding which they attribute to the enactment of a law making bottles and artificial teats available only upon the advice of a medical worker. Apparently simple, national policies of this sort can curb the impact of the improper use of the bottle.

234. Alakija, W. and F. Ukoli.
"Feeding Habits of Infants in Benin City, Nigeria." *Tropical Doctor* 10:29, 1980.
The results of a survey of 237 mothers who had contact with Benin City's health center in Nigeria show that the mothers' reasons for beginning bottle feeding follow the pattern for much of the less-developed world; that is, over half the mothers gave their reason for ceasing to breastfeed as "insufficient milk". Other reasons given were employment and health-care worker advice.

235. Almroth, E. G.
"Water Requirements of Breast-Fed Infants in a Hot Climate." *American Journal of Clinical Nutrition* 31:1154, July 1978.
The water needs of infants who are breastfeeding is the subject of this article. Although breast milk will generally supply necessary nutrients to the young infant, will the infant receive enough total liquids, especially in hot climates, from breast milk alone? The authors conclude that no additional water is generally needed unless the child is sick. Since water is often contaminated in less-developed countries, it is beneficial to know that none need be given to infants in order to supplement milk liquids in early infancy.

236. Baker, Frances L. and Joseph J. Vitale.
"Breast Versus Bottle Feeding." *Journal of Pediatrics* 92(5):864, May 1978.
The ease with which some draw conclusions from data is the issue addressed by this letter sent to a professional journal about the subject of breastfeeding and its effects on reducing morbidity in infants. The authors point to the unsatisfactory categories which are often created by researchers and to hidden assumptions which can skew results.

237. Barrell, R. A. E. and M. G. M. Rowland.
"Infant Foods as a Potential Source of Diarrhoeal Illness in Rural West Africa."
Transactions of the Royal Society of Tropical Medicine and Hygiene 73:85,
1979.
Nearly three hundred types of foods were sampled and examined for
contamination by serious bacteria such as E. coli, B. cereus, Staph
and others. Fifty-five percent of all foods contained unacceptably
high levels of E. coli during the wet season and much less during dry
seasons.

238. Barrell, R. A. E. and M. G. M. Rowland.
"Commercial Milk Products and Indigenous Weaning Foods in a Rural West
African Environment: A Bacteriological Perspective." *Journal of Hygiene*
(London) 84:191, 1980.
Two commercially prepared formulas and one native gruel were prepared in various ways which might be typical of preparation in rural
West African villages. Viable bacteria were counted after variations
in the preparations were followed. The reconstituting of the various
feeds with boiled water lowered bacterial counts. The acidified formula
appeared to reduce the multiplication rate of bacteria when it was
stored for a period of time.

239. Baumslaug, Naomi and Edward Sabin.
"Perspectives in Maternal-Infant Nutrition." Department of Health, Education
and Welfare, U. S. Government, Office of International Health, 24 pp., TAB/-
Nutrition/OIH RSSA 782-77-0138-KS, September 1978.
In this paper the authors explore the values of breastfeeding and the
reasons for the decline of breastfeeding, especially in urban areas.
While other causes are mentioned, the cause most criticized by the
writers is the promotional activities of commercial formula companies.
Education of mothers and appropriate regulation by governments are
two suggestions which the authors bring forward to deal with the
problems which they identify.

240. Bolton-Maggs, Paula H.
"Breast or Bottle." *British Medical Journal* 2(6186):371, August 11, 1979.
The author stresses that the establishment of breastfeeding by the
new mother receives comparatively little encouragement, while the
formula alternative seems to get most of the support. The setting here
is not in less-developed countries but in the United Kingdom and,
presumably, in other developed countries.

241. Briscoe, John.
"The Quantitative Effect of Infection on the Use of Food by Young Children in
Poor Countries." *American Journal of Clinical Nutrition* 32:648, March 1979.
This useful article explains the many nutritional problems created by
infections in children. Malabsorption of nutrients caused by gastrointestinal infections, changes in food intake caused by infections, and
catabolic losses are all discussed. A useful framework for evaluating
the effect of infection on food intake is also provided.

242. Brown, K. H., et al.
"Consumption of Foods and Nutrients by Weanlings in Rural Bangladesh."
American Journal of Clinical Nutrition 36:878, no date.
That breast milk plays a very important role in the nutrition of

children in countries of the less-developed world even when cereals and other nutrients are given to the children during the period from five to thirty months is borne out by this study. Over the period from five to thirty months the consumption of breast milk gradually decreased and the consumption of other solid nutrients increased. Nevertheless, breast milk nutrients still were very important to total nutrition.

243. Brown, Roy E.
"Relactation with Reference to Application in Developing Countries." *Clinical Pediatrics* 17(4):333, April 1978.
The author describes the process of relactation and argues that if women should stop breastfeeding for a time or if a natural mother should suddenly die while the child is in infancy, then the woman who has stopped breastfeeding or another woman, in the case of a deceased mother, can be induced to lactate. That process is accomplished by putting a sucking child at the breast at frequent intervals, or by chemical means. The author explains how women who were not the natural mothers of infants suckled young orphans during the Vietnam War.

244. Bwibo, Nimrod O.
Letter, University of Nairobi, Faculty of Medicine, Department of Pediatrics, April 14, 1978. Copy available at Public Policy Education Fund, Inc., 161 E. Pine St., Grove City, PA.
In this letter, Kenyan Professor Bwibo protests the portrayal of bottle feeding in Peter Krieg's controversial film, "Bottle Babies". Bwibo, who appeared in the film, states that his comments were excluded from the film, that his hospital's emphasis on hygienic education was ignored and that it propounded incorrect social connotations by showing pictures of bottles on children's graves. Labeling this film as "emotional, biased, and exaggerated", Bwibo challenges its inaccuracy and concludes by pointing out his positive relationship with Nestle by cooperating to find the best approach to infant feeding. He denies any commercialized advertising pressure, stating that his beneficial contacts with Nestle began long before the making of the film, and that his hospital is more satisfied with Nestle's practical help than with the film's "exaggerated and distorted views." Note: See Doug Johnson's response to this letter, #442.

245. Chandra, R. K.
"Breastfeeding, Growth, and Morbidity." *Nutrition Research* 1:25, 1981.
Of those infants exclusively breastfed, most achieved average growth through the third month of life. Faltering growth (judged as weight at or below the 10th percentile) was seen, however, in about 8% of the infants at age four months, 13% at five months, 22% at six months, and 33% at eight months.

246. Chase, Ann.
"Breast or Bottle." *British Medical Journal* 2(6188):492, August 25, 1979.
This letter stresses the need for the encouragement and support of the mother during the first months of her breastfeeding experience.

247. Committee on International Nutrition Programs.
"International Assistance for Maternal and Infant Nutrition in Developing Countires." Report by the Committee on International Nutrition Programs, Food and Nutrition Board, National Research Council, Washington, D.C.: National Academy of Science, August 1978.

This is the report of the consensus view from a conference of prominent nutritionists and physicians held at the request of the Office of Nutrition of the U.S. Agency for International Development. The report is reasonable in tone. The recommendations made by the conferees include the encouragement of interested governments in their own programs to promote breastfeeding and to improve nutrition in general. Also recommended is governmental aid to those national governments which want to investigate the effects of the practices of commercial vendors of formula on their own citizens. The conferees, in addition, recognized that there was a dearth of data on a number of subjects having to do with infant and family nutritional practices in less-developed countries. Conferees urge the further study of biomedical programs, cultural settings and service delivery systems.

248. Constable, Elinor.
"WHO Infant Formula Code." *Department State Bulletin* 81:34, September 1981.

Ms. Constable's statement was made following the U.S. vote against the WHO Code. Constable's position is that the U. S. opposition was due to certain ambiguities in the Code and to constitutional and legal problems. The United States, by the statement of Constable, reaffirms its support for WHO and all efforts to promote the health of children.

249. Cully, Phyllis, et al.
"Are Breast Fed Babies Still Getting a Raw Deal in Hospitals?" *British Medical Journal* 2(6195):891, October 13, 1979.

When two infant groups, one group formula fed and the other breastfed, were fed six times a day every four hours, the average intake and weight gain of the breastfed group was significantly less than that of the group artificially fed. The authors believe that such a result shows the need for more frequent feeding of breastfed babies if breastfeeding is to be encouraged.

250. Cunningham, Alan S.
"Morbidity in Breastfed and Artificially Fed Infants, Part II." *Journal of Pediatrics* 95:685, 1979.

Studying feeding practices in New York State, the author finds that breastfeeding affords protection from morbidity during the early months, and the protection increases with the duration of breastfeeding. See Part I at #067.

251. Davanzo, J. and W. P. Butz.
"Influences on Fertility and Infant Mortality in Developing Countries: The Case of Malaysia." Santa Monica, CA: The Rand Corporation, 1978.

This article, based upon a 1,200 family study in Malaysia, states that commercial infant foods help to reduce infant mortality because they are more nutritious than traditional feeds. On the other hand, commercial infant foods increase infant mortality because they discourage breastfeeding. Overall, then, the study concludes that each effect tends to offset the other. When it comes to the formulation of public policy, therefore, the authors conclude that to restrict the availability of infant formula would not benefit Malaysians.

252. Dayal, R. S.
"Current Status of Breastfeeding and Its Promotion in India." Paper presented at Pre-Congress Workshop on Breast Feeding and Supplementary Foods. Bangkok, November, 1979.
After reviewing various Indian studies of infant feeding, the author concludes that breastfeeding is most likely to be done by the lower level of socio-economic groups and by those with lower levels of education. There has been no significant decline in breastfeeding in India and the author offers various educational initiatives which will keep any decline from occurring. The article also contains data about the percentage of mothers in eleven areas who breastfed at various periods following delivery from 6 to 48 months.

253. Dobbing, John.
"Breast *Is* Best." *Nutrition Bulletin #33* 6(3):130, September 1981.
This brief editorial argues for the superiority of breastfeeding, yet notes that bottle feeding may be good for many babies.

254. "Does A Vote of 118 to 1 Mean the U.S. Was Wrong?"
Pediatrics 68(3):431, September 1981.
The writer emphasizes the lack of proper evidence in the formula feeding dispute in this short letter.

255. Dugdale, A. E.
"Infant Feeding, Growth, and Mortality: A 20-Year Study of an Australian Aboriginal Community." *Medical Journal of Australia* 2:380, 1980.
An Australian aboriginal community showed a decline in infant mortality between 1953 and 1972. Records disclosed that from 1953 to 1963 there was a statistically significant decline in breastfeeding. Infant growth and mortality did not vary according to breast versus bottle feeding in any way that was statistically significant. The decline in infant mortality was probably attributable to better and earlier use of health care services.

256. Edozien, J. C., et al.
"Medical Evaluation of the Special Supplemental Food Program for Women, Infants, and Children." *American Journal of Clinical Nutrition* 36:677, 1979.
This study on the U. S. Department of Agriculture program of food supplements given to mothers, infants and children under four years of age seems to show that birth weights were lower and mortality was higher than expected in a well-nourished population. The study raises doubts about the value of approaches like maternal supplementation. The results of the study and their application, however, are unclear for policy purposes.

257. Edson, Lee.
"Babies in Poverty: The Real Victims of the Breast/Bottle Controversy." *The Lactation Review* 4(1):21, 1979.
A special issue of this publication features an interview with Margaret

Mead. Mead says, "Your answer has to be breastfeeding plus supplementation. Never breastfeeding alone." A second twenty-page essay may be summarized in a sentence which states, "Breastfeeding may be preferable under most conditions, but bottle feeding may be the only solution at other times."

258. Ellestad-Sayad, Judith, et al.
"Breast-Feeding Protects Against Infection in Indian Infants." *Canadian Medical Association Journal* 120(3):295, February 3, 1979.
Based upon a study of Indian communities in Canada, the authors conclude that breastfeeding is especially important to social groups whose morbidity and mortality are higher than average. In this study, breastfeeding served as a protective practice against disease. In addition, the cost of breastfeeding was lower than artificial feeding.

259. Fallot, Mary E., John L. Boyd III and Frank Oski.
"Breastfeeding Reduces Incidence of Hospital Admissions for Infection in Infants." *Pediatrics* 65(6):1121, June 1980.
The conclusion of this study, based on collected data and existing hospital records in central New York State, is that morbidity tends to be lower in exclusively breastfed infants than among formula fed infants.

260. Foman, Samuel J. and Ronald G. Strauss.
"Nutrient Deficiencies in Breast-Fed Infants." *New England Journal of Medicine* 299(7):355, August 1978.
Though human milk is a "superb food" for infants, it is neither a perfect nor a complete food. This editorial outlines in easy-to-understand terms the need for supplementation of certain vitamins and minerals, even when mothers producing the breast milk are healthy and well-nourished.

261. Fomon, Samuel, et al.
"Recommendations for Feeding Normal Infants." *Pediatrics* 63(1):52, January 1979.
The authors recommend breastfeeding with supplements of iron, vitamin D, and fluoride. Occasional infant formula feeding is permissible. "Beikost", that is, foods other than breast milk or formula should not be introduced until 5 to 6 months. Between 5 and 6 months an iron-fortified dry cereal should be introduced. There is no reason to discontinue breastfeeding before 18 to 24 months of age, but other foods, commercial or home-prepared, should be introduced gradually.

262. Food and Agricultural Organization of the United Nations.
"Cultivating Malnutrition". Food and Agricultural Organization Study, "World Hunger: Implications for U.S. Policies About the Effects of U. S. Trade and Investment on the Hungry." In: *Background Paper #38.* Washington, D.C.: FAO, August 1979.
This document is a "pre-publication" release of a study by the FAO. The authors suggest that trade relations with developing countries be directly related to how well a given country distributes its own resources to its people, particularly in the area of food distribution. Mexico is used as an example. The United States should not buy

natural gas from Mexico, the authors say, until it does a better job of distributing food.

263. Forsum, E. and B. Lonnerdal.
"Effect of Protein Intake on Protein and Nitrogen Composition of Breastmilk." *American Journal of Clinical Nutrition* 33:1809, 1980.
This technical article on the effects of low and high protein diets on the contents of different nitrogen-containing substances in breast milk was based on a study of Swedish mothers who were in full lactation. Certain concentrations of nitrogen, protein and nonprotein nitrogen were significantly higher for the mothers who took the higher protein diet. Other outputs were not significantly different.

264. Gaskin, Ina May.
"Nestle Boycott." *Journal of Nurse-Midwifery* 26(1):39, January/February 1981.
In this letter to the editor, the writer disputes some of the earlier points made by Carol Pinckney. Some of the response is personal and not very helpful, but other arguments in favor of opposition to formula feeding are clearly presented.

265. Gilmore, H. E. and T. W. Rowland.
"Clinical Malnutrition in Breast-Fed Infants." *American Journal of Diseases in Childhood* 132:885, 1978.
The authors report three cases of dehydrated and marasmic children, 13 to 30 days old and weighing less than they weighed at birth. All had been breastfed. The authors counsel careful instruction, support and follow-up for newly nursing mothers. It is incorrect to presume that lactation is adequate in every case.

266. Gordon, A. G.
"Breast Is Best, But Bottle Is Worst." *Lancet* 2(8238):151, July 18, 1981.
Gordon argues in this footnoted letter to the editor that bottle feeding, if done properly, that is, without the infant supine, will not produce the many harmful results which are attributed to it. "Bottle-propping" can cause the milk and other fluids to run into the eustachian tubes and pool in the ear where, briefly put, organisms can breed. This unique view is worthy of consideration since it seems to call into question the position that disease results largely from the ingestion of harmful bacteria.

267. Graham, George G.
"Comments on the World Health Organization's 'International Code' of Marketing of Breastmilk Substitutes." *American Journal of Diseases in Childhood* 135:892, October 1981.
The writer explains that the WHO deliberations failed to show an association between the marketing of formula and a decline in breast-feeding. Moreover, observers with varying experiences see the formula needs of infants differently. In certain parts of the world, breastfeeding is maintained but infant mortality is high. In certain areas of the developing world, clean water and some refrigeration are coming into use. There, the choice of formula or breastfeeding should be the mother's. In other areas, formula is too expensive for use as a supplement but many native weaning foods are also inadequate. The issues are

complex and will not be solved by stronger attacks on multinational enterprises.

268. Greiner, Ted and Michael Latham.
"Infant Feeding Practices in St. Vincent and Factors Which Affect Them." *West Indian Medical Journal* 30:8, 1981.
Over 190 mothers of St. Vincent in the Caribbean were interviewed as to the infant feeding methods they practiced. Over 90% breastfed their infants. Seventy-five percent introduced supplementary milk before one month and about the same percentage fed their infants a supplement of gruel by four months. The authors state that St. Vincent has the highest infant and child mortality rate in the English-speaking Caribbean. The factors which influenced feeding practices could not be determined by the authors.

269. Gueri, Miguel, Peter Justsum and R. Hoyte.
"Breast-Feeding Practices in Trinidad." *Bulletin of the Pan American Health Organization* 12(4):316, 1978.
This study concluded that breastfeeding in Trinidad is given up by the fourth month in many cases, and that this may lead to malnutrition. The authors make extensive use of charts and tables.

270. Gueri, Miguel, Peter Justsum and Alison White.
"Evaluation of a Breast-Feeding Campaign in Trinidad." *Bulletin of the Pan American Health Organization* 12(2):112, 1978.
In 1974, in Trinidad, a women's group, with technical assistance, launched a campaign promoting breastfeeding. The group used posters, and newspaper, television and radio advertisements. This article, based upon hospital interviews, discusses the campaign and its impact upon mothers. There was a positive correlation between the ads and the choice by women to avoid bottle feeding and to choose breastfeeding.

271. Gunn, R. A., et al.
"Bottle Feeding as a Risk Factor for Cholera in Infants." *Lancet* ii:730, 1979.
In the Persian Gulf country of Bahrain, a study revealed that there was a higher incidence of El Tor cholera cases among infants in the six to eleven month age group who had been primarily bottle fed as opposed to those who had been primarily breastfed during the week before the onset of the illness.

272. Gussler, J. D. and L. H. Briesemeister.
"The Insufficient Milk Syndrome: A Biocultural Explanation." *Medical Anthropology* 4:3, 1980.
Professors Gussler and Briesemeister present a well-reasoned analysis of what they call the insufficient milk syndrome. Mothers in the less-developed world give the insufficiency of milk as the most common explanation for not continuing breastfeeding. The authors argue that the effects of urban culture are really most often to blame for the circumstances which make breastfeeding difficult. Breastfeeding declines have not occurred generally in rural areas of the less-developed world, but have been evident in urban areas.

273. Hall, Barbara.
"Uniformity of Human Milk." *American Journal of Clinical Nutrition* 32:304, February 1979.
The evidence presented here and in several other reports on human milk composition which are referred to by the author shows that human milk is uniform in its composition. When it varies, the variations are not random.

274. Hansen, J. D. L.
"Breast Versus Bottle Feeding." *South African Medical Journal* 53(12):432, March 25, 1978.
This letter by a professor in the Department of Pediatrics at the University of Witwatersand in South Africa counsels the need for improved collection of data on feeding practices and the alteration of hospital practices of keeping mothers and infants separated for a time after birth.

275. Helman, Gerald.
"U.S. Statement on WHO Infant Formula by Ambassador Gerald Helman." Geneva, May 20, 1981.
This statement mentions a few technical objections that the United States government has to the WHO Code.

276. Hide, David, Helen Graham and Carolyn Jones.
"Breast or Bottle." *British Medical Journal* 2(6192):733, September 22, 1979.
This letter to the editor refers to the experience which the writers have had on the Isle of Wight with the encouragement of mothers who are breastfeeding. They conclude that the pressures and demands of modern living make breastfeeding very difficult for mothers and observe that the excuse given by most women — inadequate lactation — may be a true explanation.

277. Hirschman, C. and M. Butler.
"Trends and Differentials in Breast-Feeding: An Update." *Demography* 18:39, February 1981.
This scholarly article concerns itself with breastfeeding habits of United States' women. The evidence gathered shows the continuation of a downward trend in breastfeeding among American women. The study notes that the groups most likely to breastfeed are women who are college graduates, and who are professionals, or who are married to professionals. The article is important as an indicator of maternal preferences among a highly literate, informed group of consumers.

278. Ho, Zhi-Chien.
"Breastfeeding in Xinhui District in South China." *U.N. University Food and Nutrition Bulletin* 3:42, 1981.
By measuring weight of infants, two to eight months after birth, the author determined the average breast milk output of mothers. The data was gathered in South China, Guangdong Province. The monthly weight gains of infants were below the United Kindgom standard from three months of age on.

279. Hopkins, H.
"Next to Mother's Milk, There's Infant Formula." *FDA Consumer* (Food and Drug Administration, U.S. Government) 14:11, July/August 1980.
Hopkins contends that artificially created formula can be deficient in some important respects, and refers to the specific cases of formula brands Neo-Mull-Soy and Cho-free. Ironically, the manufacturer, Syntex Laboratories, had ordered that salt not be added to these formulas in response to consumerist agitation that baby foods were often excessively salted. Salt is necessary for the infant and its absence from these brands caused deficiency symptoms in a small number of cases. This article also contains a brief insert on the commercial development of formula following the development of evaporated milk.

280. Huffman, S., et al.
"Breast Feeding Patterns in Rural Bangladesh." *American Journal of Clinical Nutrition* 33:19, 1980.
Mothers in rural Bangladesh breastfeed on median average about 30 months. About 75% of the women with children still living were breast-feeding at 2½ years postpartum.

281 Jelliffe, D. B.
"Feeding Young Infants in Developing Countries." *Journal of Tropical Pediatrics and Environmental Child Health* 24(4):155, August 1978.
Jelliffe presents the view that in addition to certain kinds of reactions to cow's milk and other disturbances to health, the feeding of artificial milk products to infants in the Third World has been a part of the reason for an increase in malnutrition, morbidity and mortality among these infants. The promotional actions of the infant formula companies are condemned by the article and, though mention is made of industry efforts to develop a code of ethics, the article sees the resulting code as ambiguous and the companies as evasive.

282. Jelliffe, D. B. and E. F. P. Jelliffe.
"The Volume and Composition of Human Milk in Poorly Nourished Countries. A Review." *American Journal of Clinical Nutrition* 31:492, 1978.
The authors review information about the quantity and composition of breast milk from developed and less-developed countries. They emphasize the problems of measuring breast milk output, but, nevertheless, reach certain conclusions. For well-nourished mothers exclusive breastfeeding is adequate for the first six months of the child's life. Milk output for poorly nourished mothers is often below optimum. As for composition, the milk of poorly nourished mothers may have lower levels of vitamin A and other vitamins as well as lower fat content.

283. Jelliffe, D. B. and E. F. P. Jelliffe.
Human Milk in the Modern World. Oxford: Oxford University Press, 1978.
The authors are two of the leading experts on human milk and infant feeding in the world. This work explores the various aspects of lactation, from physiology to economics. Discussed, among other things, are the changes that have occurred in breastfeeding in Western urban societies as well as in non-Western societies. An extensive bibliography is included.

284. Jelliffe, D. B. and E. F. P. Jelliffe.
"The Weanling's Dilemma." *Lancet* p. 611, March 18, 1978.
This letter takes issue with some of the points made by Dr. Rowland and disagrees with certain interpretations put on the data. The letter shows the differences which can arise even between two scientists.

285. Jelliffe, D. B. and E. F. P. Jelliffe.
"The Infant Food Industry." *Lancet* p. 263, July 29, 1978.
This letter is a response to the statement by ICIFI which *The Lancet* had earlier published. The writers argue that the Code adopted by ICIFI is ambiguous and that changes in promotional efforts by the infant food industry have come about because of the work of critics. The problem of continuously monitoring promotional practices still remains.

286. Jelliffe, D. B. and E. F. P. Jelliffe.
"Feeding Young Infants in Developing Countries: Comments on the Future Situation and Future Needs." *Studies in Family Planning* 9(8):227, August 1978.
In this statement, the often-quoted husband and wife team of Dr. Derrick Jelliffe and E. F. Patrice Jelliffe comment on the introduction of formula and breast milk substitutes into less-developed countries. The statement to which others so often refer is that some ten million cases annually of marasmus and diarrhea are related in part to inadequate bottle feeding. Though the statement has been challenged by others, it, nevertheless, appears in much material of the popular campaign. The Jelliffes plainly oppose the promotional practices of the formula companies. The publication contains certain proposals for reform. Formula companies should concentrate on cheaper, minimally advertised formulas and supplemental weaning food, and upon low-cost maternal dietary supplements.

287. Jelliffe, D. B. and E. F. P. Jelliffe.
"Early Infant Nutrition Breastfeeding." In: Winick, M., ed. Nutrition: Pre- and Postnatal Development. New York: Plenum Press, 1979; p. 229.
The authors suggest that poorly nourished mothers should receive supplemental food during pregnancy in order to bring their milk production to an optimum level. Breastfeeding and formula feeding for children from birth to nine months and from nine months to two years are discussed.

288. Jelliffe, D. B. and E. F. P. Jelliffe.
"Successful Breast Feeding in the Ivory Coast." *American Journal of Clinical Nutrition* 33:6, January 1980.
This letter is a response to the findings of Edgar Lauber and Michael Reinhart in the *American Journal of Clinical Nutrition* 32:1159, May 1979, infra at #295. The authors call the Lauber/Reinhart conclusions "modest", and say that the researchers have proven that exclusive breastfeeding is adequate for infants of less-than-optimally nourished mothers during the first five to six months.

289. Kardjati, S., et al.
"Feeding Practices, Nutritional Status and Mortality in Pre-School Children in Rural East Java, Indonesia." *Tropical Georgia Medicine* 30:359, 1978.
In rural East Java (Indonesia) a study was made by random sampling

of approximately 2,300 infants and children from birth to four years. Between 80-90% were either partially or exclusively breastfed for the first eighteen months. There was no decline in breastfeeding over the last two decades, as reported, although some regional differences, district to district, in the duration of lactation were observed. Supplementation generally occurred in the early months of feeding.

290. Kent, Mary M.
   "Breastfeeding in the Developing World: Current Patterns and Implications for Future Trends." *World Fertility Survey* (2), Population Reference Bureau, Inc., 1981.
   Nineteen developing countries are the subject of this survey. The lengthy and scholarly report, which is the result of the survey, concludes that the percentage of mothers breastfeeding in Asian countries was on average over 90% in all but two countries. In Kenya, the only African country surveyed, 96% of children were breastfed with weaning occurring at approximately thirteen months. In the Latin American countries surveyed, the breastfeeding was on average over 90% in all but two countries. The data analysis is very well done. Due to the unsupported accusations of a general and precipitous decline in breastfeeding, this survey should be consulted and used. The results are similar to those of the WHO Collaborative Study on Breastfeeding.

291. Knodel, J. and N. Debavalya.
   "Breast-Feeding Trends in Thailand and Their Demographic Impact." *Intercom* p. 8, March 1981.
   A sociologist and demographer team have produced a most interesting article on the trend of breastfeeding in Thailand. The duration of breastfeeding has declined in Thailand in both rural and urban areas during the period 1969 to 1979. This is one of the few longitudinal studies measuring results under specific conditions for an extended time period. At the close of the period studied, however, the duration of breastfeeding was still relatively long — 17.5 months for rural women and 8.4 months for urban women. The authors are also surprised to find that a reduction of breastfeeding has not been accompanied by an increase in mortality and fertility.

292. Korcok, Milan.
   "Health Problems of Developing Nations — Part I: A Western Solution?" *Canadian Medical Association Journal* 120(4):471, February 17, 1979.
   Western solutions to the health problems of less-developed countries may not always be the most effective ways to deal with the problems presented. This is the thesis of an interesting article which only mentions milk products in passing. Insight can be gained, however, from the comments about WHO.

293. Lambert, Julian.
   "Bottle-Feeding Legislation in Papua, New Guinea." *Journal of Human Nutrition* 34(1):23, 1980.
   In 1977, legislation was introduced in Papua, New Guinea which restricted the sale of infant feeding bottles and teats. In order to obtain a bottle, a mother had to present a prescription to a pharmacy. The prescription could be issued only after the health worker deter-

mined that such a feeding method was in the best interests of the child and that the mother was familiar with proper sanitation and formula preparation procedures. A decline in artificial feeding can be seen between 1975 and 1979, the period during which this legislation and other retrictions were put in place.

294. Larsen, Spencer A. and Daryl R. Homer.
"Relation of Breast Versus Bottle Feeding to Hospitalization for Gastroenteritis in Middle Class U. S. Population." *The Journal of Pediatrics* 92(32):417, March 1978.
According to this article, recent studies have shown much lower morbidity and mortality from gastroenteritis in breastfed versus bottle fed infants in under-developed countries with poor sanitation. In order to test those findings in the United States, the authors studied infants in a California location. The data strongly indicates, according to the authors, that breastfeeding plays a major role in protection against intestinal infections.

295. Lauber, Edgar and Michael Reinhardt.
"Studies on the Quality of Breast Milk During 23 Months of Lactation in a Rural Community of the Ivory Coast." *American Journal of Clinical Nutrition* 32:1159, May 1979.
Thirty-three women gave breast milk samples over a period of twenty-three months in the Ivory Coast. Bottle feeding was virtually unknown though starchy supplements were given in addition to breast milk from six months on. The mothers' diets consisted mainly of yam, plantain, and cassava and were poor in protein and fat. The authors were concerned with the lipid content of the milk since the importance of lipids to normal brain development has been stressed by several authors. Lipid composition remained virtually constant. Infants grew well for the first five months, but thereafter their growth curves were unsatisfactory by Western standards.

296. Lucas, A. and J. D. Baum.
"No Raw Deal for Breast Fed Babies." *British Medical Journal* 2(6199):1221, November 10, 1979.
The authors of this letter, who are members of a department of pediatrics, say that breastfed babies may take in less milk than bottle fed babies during the first five days of life. They also point out that sucking response is different for those given infant formula than for those who are breastfed.

297. Mardones-Santander, F.
"History of Breastfeeding in Chile." *U.N. University Food and Nutrition Bulletin* 1:15, 1979.
This study concludes that breastfeeding declined in Chile in the 1930s or earlier, probably during the movement of people from rural to urban locations which occurred from the 1900s to the 1930s. Breastfeeding as exclusive nourishment for the infants' first three months has remained rather constant.

298. Marshall, L. B. and M. A. C. Marshall.
"Breasts, Bottles and Babies: Historical Changes in Infant Feeding Practices in a Micronesian Village." *Ecology of Food and Nutrition* 8:241, 1979.
This study covered the period from 1945 to 1975 in a Micronesian

village (Moen Island). The use of commercial infant formula increased and exclusive breastfeeding declined. Reasons for the mothers' choice of formula as opposed to exclusive breastfeeding, in relative order of importance, were: convenience, employment or seeking an education. Some mothers were too tired after work to breastfeed. "Inadequate breastmilk" accounted for less than 10% of the responses. The presence of Americans on the island, as teachers, health professionals and mothers, appeared to influence the movement away from breastfeeding. No extensive advertising of formula was done there in the period studied.

299. Martinez, Gilbert A. and John P. Nalezienski.
"The Recent Trend in Breast Feeding." *Pediatrics* 64(5):689, 1979.
The authors point to survey-obtained research data which shows that after a decline in breastfeeding in the United States from 1955 to 1971 there has been a resurgence of breastfeeding from 1971 to 1979. Much data is offered by the authors for those interested in the seemingly simple but actually very complex problem.

300. Martinez, Gilbert A. and John P. Nalezienski.
"1980 Update: The Recent Trend in Breastfeeding." *Pediatrics* 67(2):260, February 1981.
The authors, using mailed surveys, asked mothers about their infant feeding practices from the period 1955-1979. The findings are that from 1951 to 1971 breastfeeding in the United States was on the decline. From 1971 to 1979, however, there was a resurgence of breastfeeding. The increase in incidence was not limited to higher income or better educated mothers.

301. May, Charles D.
"The 'Infant Formula Controversy': A Notorious Threat to Reason in Matters of Health." *Pediatrics* 68(3), September 1981.
This letter, in the commentary portion of the journal, contains many worthwhile points, but in essence Dr. May stresses that scientific evidence has not been produced which links the decline in breastfeeding, which has occurred at some places, with the availability of baby formula.

302. Monckeberg, Fernando.
"Crying over the Spilled Milk." *Creces* p. 25, 1981.
This writer, whose original article is in Spanish, argues that the problem of Third World infant malnutrition is much more complicated than the opponents of formula feeding are making it. He states that environmental contamination produces babies who are malnourished even if breastfed. This occurs because of such things as flies on the body of the mother and on the baby's skin and hands.

303. Pelto, G. H.
"Perspectives on Infant Feeding: Decision Making and Ecology." *Food and Nutrition Bulletin* 3:16, 1981.
Traditional cultures follow breastfeeding practices which are consistent with its views of child training and other social, economic and cultural characteristics. The author also reviews breastfeeding trends

in the West and emphasizes that many factors influence decisions, but the decisions reached are rational in that the decision-maker weighs various conditions and alternatives before the choice is made.

304. Pittard, William B., III.
"Breast Milk Immunology." *American Journal of Diseases in Childhood* 133:83, January 1979.
The author discusses in technical terms the immunoprotective properties of human milk. Although it is known that B-lymphocytes produce antibodies and that a theory has been developed about this process, much remains to be investigated in this important area.

305. Popkin, Barry M.
"Economic Determinants of Breastfeeding Behavior: The Case of Rural Households in Laguna, Philippines." In: Mosely, W. H. ed. Nutrition and Human Reproduction. New York: Plenum Press, 1978; p. 461.
Over 570 households in the Philippines were surveyed to determine what characteristics were associated with breastfeeding choices. Predictably, working mothers had a lower probability of breastfeeding, although if they did breastfeed, they often fed longer than non-working mothers. Also considered to have had an impact on the mother were such things as the likelihood of supporting help for the mother in the household, urbanization, activities of food processors, the beliefs and preferences of the mother, and other factors.

306. Popkin, Barry M., et al.
"Breast-Feeding Practices in Low Income Countries: Patterns and Determinants." *Carolina Population Center Papers* No. 11, October 1979.
This long and technical paper reviews patterns and changes in the extent and duration of breastfeeding in low per-capita-income nations. The authors say that in some areas of the world a decline in the proportion of children being breastfed and a decline in the duration of the breastfeeding can be shown but that "there is strong evidence of continuing almost universal breastfeeding for the first year of life in most Asian and African countries." The study carefully reviews the possible determinants that may be contributing to changing patterns of infant feeding.

307. Post, James E. and Edward Baer.
"Analyzing Complex Policy Problems: The Social Performance of the International Infant Formula Industry." In: Lee Preston, ed. Research in Corporate Social Performance and Policy Vol. 2., Greenwich, CT: JAI Press, Inc., 1980; p. 157.
The authors use the infant formula controversy as a case by which to observe and categorize corporate responses to scrutiny of international operations. The writers do point out, among other things, that in their study of Colombia, there was no simple answer to the question of whether the activities of infant formula manufacturers induced women to abandon breastfeeding, thereby leading to increased morbidity and mortality among children. The authors say that structural factors, namely profit seeking, make it difficult for member firms of an industry to restrict their own competitive actions. Also, the writers observe that public issue controversies go through several identifiable and predictable stages.

308. Preston, Thomas Scott.

"Innocents Abroad: Infant Food Technology at the Law's Frontier." 20 *Virginia Journal of International Law* 617, Spring 1980.

The infant formula controversy presented problems to the international law community. The author reviews some of these problems in a thorough way. Existing regulatory agencies and entities cannot very easily prohibit formula sales. The author discusses the proposed Infant Nutrition Act, which, had it been enacted by the United States, would have prohibited the sale by American companies of infant formula in less-developed countries. Such national legislation, however, would not have controlled the sale of formula by the companies of other countries. Preston proposes that regulating be done by appropriate international organs like the United Nations. The author seems to consider no other alternatives and is obviously well-convinced that formula feeding should be controlled and not left to market forces.

309. Raphael, Dana, ed.

Breastfeeding and Food Policy in a Hungry World. New York: Academic Press, 1978.

This book contains many useful articles about the anthropology of breastfeeding which were given as papers at the International Conference on Human Lactation conducted by the Human Lactation Center and the New York Academy of Sciences, in March 1977. Papers include those by Margaret Mead and editor Raphael. The papers discuss the system of folk beliefs and practices that influence the mother in the feeding of her child, the use of weaning and supplementary foods, and the social networks of support for breastfeeding mothers and how they may be adversely affected by urbanization, among other things.

310. Raphael, Dana, ed.

"Breastfeeding and Weaning Among the Poor." *The Lactation Review* 3(1), 1978.

The Center for Human Lactation studies infant feeding habits worldwide. The findings of this report are that infant mortality decreased in the three decades prior to 1973 when food prices generally rose. Breast milk is the best food for infants for the first three months, but after three months it should not be the exclusive source of nutrients. Supplementation is important. Mixed feeding is almost universal in traditional cultures.

311. Relucio-Clavano, Natividad.

"How Can Hospitals Encourage Breastfeeding: Example from the Philippines." Reprint, New York: Interfaith Center on Corporate Responsibility, c. 1981.

The author explains how she implemented a change from widespread formula feeding, within Baguio General Hospital in the northern Philippines, to a greater use of breastfeeding. Attached are hospital procedures to be followed in establishing an in-hospital breastfeeding program.

312. Rosenberg, Irwin H.

"Resumé of the Discussion on Direct Nutrition Interventions." *American Journal of Clinical Nutrition* 31:2083, November 1978.

This is a summary of a discussion on the question of "Direct Nutrition

Interventions" which includes many experts on infant nutrition. The discussants recognize the desirability of breastfeeding but also the social pressures in a developing economy for the woman to work. Also discussed are maternal supplementation, the appropriate point for infant supplementation, and the proper way to use birth-weight as an indicator of nutritional needs.

313. Rowland, M. G. M., R. A. E. Barrell and R. G. Whitehead.
"Bacterial Contamination in Traditional Gambian Weaning Foods." *Lancet* p. 136, January 21, 1978.
That traditional weaning foods used for young infants in a typical West African village can be as hazardous bacteriologically as commercial milk products, is the finding of this important piece of research. Supplemental gruels were prepared and tested for bacteria. The results are noted.

314. Rowland, M. G. M. and R. A. E. Barrell.
"Infant Foods as a Potential Source of Diarrhoeal Illness in Rural West Africa." *Transactions of the Royal Society of Tropical Medicine and Hygiene* 73(1):85, 1979.
This study emphasizes the danger of storing native weaning foods for long periods of time at ambient temperatures. Foods not immediately consumed were found to be hazardous much of the time and almost always so after eight hours.

315. Rowland, M. G. M., A. A. Paul and R. G. Whitehead.
"Lactation and Infant Nutrition." *British Medical Bulletin* 37:77, 1981.
When is lactation adequate? What is *normal* growth for an infant? These are questions which the authors address in this comparison between Cambridge, England infants and infants of Gambia. The authors raise questions about the international weight standards for infants at three months. They may be too low. Supplementation in the industrialized West need not occur until four months, but in the less-developed world, supplements may be necessary at two to three months of age.

316. Sauls, H. S.
"Potential Effect of Demographic and Other Variables in Studies Comparing Morbidity of Breastfed and Bottlefed Babies." *Pediatrics* 64:523, October 1979.
Dr. Sauls asserts that studies to date which attempt to relate infant morbidity to the use of formula as opposed to breastfeeding have overlooked the confounding differences inherent in the sample. In plain language this means that mothers' attitudes, access to health care, and the condition of the child may all influence the morbidity of the child. In such cases, the morbidity is improperly being attributed solely to formula feeding. This is a very important article in untangling the many logical and scientific questions of the formula dispute.

317. Schapp, Paula.
"The Case for Strict Liability in the Infant Formula Industry." 6 *Brooklyn Journal of International Law* 88, Spring 1980.
The author is advocating the use of strict liability law in less-developed countries to combat the misuse of formula. Such liability without fault

is possible realistically only in countries with well developed, wealthy enterprises. She seems to recognize the unlikelihood of her proposal but calls for an international conference on the subject. The products of infant formula companies are not inherently dangerous, and, labeled with proper warnings, it seems virtually impossible to imagine strict liability rules being applied.

318. Scrimshaw, Nevin S. and B. Underwood.
"Timely and Appropriate Complementary Feeding of the Breast-Fed Infant —An Overview." *U.N. University Food and Nutrition Bulletin* 2:19, 1980.
The initiation of breastfeeding presents little problem for most mothers in developing countries. Continuing the breastfeeding for the appropriate time is more of a problem. External factors which interfere with breastfeeding should be reduced. On the other hand, mothers should be warned about the dangers of exclusive breastfeeding for too long a period. Proper supplementary feeding is important to infant growth. The transitional weaning period presents the greatest danger to the Third World infant because the traditional weaning foods are prepared from the family's existing foods which do not contain adequate nutrients. The use of commercial infant formulas as replacements for traditional weaning foods is to be invited where the people using them have adequate resources. An outright prohibition of commercial foods might actually force users to return to poor quality local foods.

319. Scrimshaw, Nevin S.
"Code Not Cure." *Nutrition Today* p. 11, July/August 1981.
The author reviews briefly the steps which led up to the adoption of the May 1981 WHO Code of Marketing for Breastmilk Substitutes, explaining the many drafts and consultations through which the Code went. He argues that the problem of infant feeding in the less-developed world will not be solved by the WHO Code. The trend away from breastfeeding antedates commercial promotion and the social and economic factors are still the most important determinants of breastfeeding practices. The author also states that good quality formulas must be available for those who need them.

320. Sethi, S. P.
"A Conceptual Framework for Environmental Analysis of Social Issues and Evaluations of Business Response Patterns." *Academy of Management Review* 4(1), January 1979.
The author analyzes the stages during a dispute between a business enterprise and various groups which are critical of that enterprise. The author believes that there is (1) a pre-problem stage during which adverse effects result from the business' activities but are not yet diagnosed, (2) an identification stage where the "problem" comes to light, (3) a remedy and relief stage and (4) a preventive stage at which attempts are made to prevent recurrence. The Nestle controversy is cited as an example of these stages in a dispute, although the writer does not have the benefit of post-1979 developments.

321. Sethi, S. P.
"Public Consequences of Private Action: The Marketing of Infant Formula in Less Developed Countries." *California Management Review* 21(4):35, Summer 1979.
This article asks whether or not firms dealing with infant formula in

alien environments over a period of time can avoid practical, ethical difficulties. The author argues that in order to avoid scandal or charges of being unethical or exploitive, firms of this type must adjust their marketing techniques to changing circumstances as problems arise so that private differences do not escalate into public issues.

322. Sibert, R., H. Jadhav and S. G. Inbaras.
"Maternal and Fetal Nutrition in South India." *British Medical Journal* 1:1517, 1978.
The authors found a significant correlation between the nutrition and general health of mothers and the weight and health of the newborn child. The study was of mothers and their infants in southern India.

323. Strauss, Ronald G.
"More of Breast Versus Bottle Feeding and the Incidence of Illness." *Journal of Pediatrics* 93(4):726, October 1978.
This is one of many letters in serious journals raising questions about the methodology of various scientists who were attempting to show a correlation between breastfeeding and the lowering of the incidence of gastroenteritis in infants.

324. Steady, Filomina Chioma.
"Infant Feeding in Developing Countries: Combatting the Multinationals' Imperative." *Journal of Tropical Pediatrics* 27(4):215, August 1981.
When the author explains the scientific advantages of breastfeeding, she contributes to the understanding of the pertinent issues. Unfortunately, the article also makes some unsubstantiated statements which detract from her overall effect. For example, the formula companies are said to be under an imperative of maximizing profits at all costs, even the cost of human life. The author also rejects the distinction between supplementation and initial feeding, a distinction that has widespread support in scientific literature.

325. Stockwell, Serena.
"Anthropologists Question Whether Ads Discourage Breastfeeding." *National Health* December 1979.
This article presents the reader with yet another viewpoint on the questions of formula feeding. The author quotes nutritional anthropologist Norge Jerome who charges INFACT with using a double standard. The author says that Third World mothers are not easily swayed by advertising and that the choices they make are most often based upon certain trade-offs and the measuring of certain conveniences. The article also quotes Dana Raphael and suggests that the idea that women in less-developed countries generally choose between the breast and the bottle is a Western notion.

326. Surjono, D., et al.
"Bacterial Contamination and Dilution of Milk in Infant Feeding Bottles." *Journal of Tropical Pediatrics* 26:58, 1980.
This study, done in Indonesia, reveals that improper preparation of infant food leads to gross bacterial contamination and that incorrect formula strength occurs in a substantial proportion of cases using bottle feeds. The authors want to encourage breastfeeding wherever

possible, but greater attention should be paid to mothers who are using bottle feeding improperly.

327. Thomson, Peter.
"The Infant Food Industry." *Lancet* 2(8086):421, August 19, 1978.
Mr. Thomson says that with 25 million advertisements per year the only real way to restrain advertisers is by self-regulation. He points to successful kinds of self-regulation in the professions and urges that similar self-monitoring devices be created to govern the sales of formula worldwide.

328. Tripp, J. H.
"Infant Feeding Practices: A Cause for Concern." *British Medical Journal* 2(6192):707, September 1979.
Even in Western developed countries advice to parents on substitutes for cow's milk, such as goat's milk or soya-based products, deserves the careful scrutiny of physicians and nutrition experts. That such substitutes may be insufficient in various ways is the main point of this article.

329. United States Department of State.
"A.I.D. Infant Feeding Programs in the Third World." *Bureau of Public Affairs, Public Information Series*, June 1981.
This publication briefly outlines various programs and efforts of the Agency for International Development, designed to promote breast-feeding and safe infant feeding practices in less-developed countries. Some of the programs use direct education of medical professionals. Others provide aid to South American and African countries to allow their governments to make studies of infant feeding practices within their own borders. Still other grants are to pro-breastfeeding groups to encourage breastfeeding in the Third World.

330. United States Department of State.
Bureau of Public Affairs, Public Information Series, June 1981.
Assistant Secretary for International Organization Affairs, Elliott Abrams, gives a good summary of the principal reasons for the U.S. vote against the WHO Code. Abrams stresses that the United States is committed to breastfeeding, but that the Code as proposed raises questions of antitrust and certain issues of intrusion into corporate and individual decisions which makes its support impossible for the United States.

331. United States House Committee on Foreign Affairs.
"Marketing and Promotion of Infant Formula In Developing Countries. Subcommittee on International Economic Policy and Trade: Hearings, January 30 and February 11, 1980. 1980 iv+ 184 p. Tables (96th Congress, Second Session) PA — Washington, D.C.
This is one of several House or Senate hearings conducted in order to determine what U.S. response should be to formula feeding sales by American companies to less-developed countries.

332. United States Senate Committee on Human Resources.
"Marketing and Promotion of Infant Formula in the Developing Nations."

Subcommittee of Health and Scientific Research, 1978; Hearing, May 23, 1978. 1978 vi+ 1498 p. Bibls., Il., Tables, Charts (95th Congress, Second Session) PA —Washington, D.C.

332-A. Ballarin, Oswaldo.
"Statement of Oswaldo Ballarin, Chairman of Nestle-Brazil to the U.S. Subcommittee on Health and Scientific Research, May 23, 1978."
Dr. Ballarin's statement and questioning by a U.S. Senate Subcommittee reveal the tactics and content of the early position taken by Nestle. Ballarin offered the view that much of the opposition to formula marketing was to be found in the efforts of an international church group to undermine the free enterprise system. Senators Kennedy and Chaffee oppose Ballarin on the many statements he makes during the hearing. It is obvious that their views are at odds with his.

332-B. Cox, David O.
"Summary Statement of Abbott Laboratories on the Role of Prepared Infant Formulas in the Third World, Presented to the Senate Subcommittee on Health and Scientific Research, May 23, 1978."
Cox presents Ross Laboratories' (a subsidiary of Abbott Laboratories) role in the sale of infant formula in the Third World. He notes that while everyone agrees that there is room for improvement in this process, the definition of the scope and nature of the problem is not clear. He notes further that his firm has an internal code for marketing, which is included in the record of the proceedings.

332-C. Margulies, Leah.
"Marketing and Promotion of Infant Formula and the Decline of Breast-Feeding in Underdeveloped Countries." Hearing, excerpted from detailed testimony submitted to the Subcommittee on Health and Scientific Research of the Committee of Human Resources, May 23, 1978.
This testimony emphasizes the data collected from various countries, mostly in South America, that formula companies were indeed promoting infant formula and that the formula was the cause of infant disease because it could not be prepared properly. Much testimony is anecdotal and does not indicate how widespread the problem referred to has become.

332-D. Post, James E.
"Testimony Before the U.S. Subcommittee on Health and Scientific Research of the Committee on Human Resources, May 23, 1978."
Although Post states that hard data is not available, he argues that the industry sees the market for formula in the less-developed countries as an important potential market. He also testifies that the firms involved have no real dedication to self-regulation through codes. Finally, he states that the marketing of infant formula produces no inherent benefits for the peoples of developing nations.

332-E. Sprole, Frank A.
"Summary of Testimony by Frank A. Sprole, Vice Chairman of the Board, Bristol-Myers Company, before the U.S. Senate Subcommittee on Health and Scientific Research." May 23, 1978.
The statement of one of the infant formula company executives is

interesting largely because of its reference to the discontinuation of mothercraft workers. The testimony reveals that physicians and health workers from less-developed countries often opposed the discontinuation of such workers.

332-F. Stafford, John R.
"Statement of Wyeth International, A Subsidiary of American Home Products Corp. before the Senate Subcommittee on Health and Scientific Research, Senate Committee on Human Resources, May 23, 1978."
One of many statements made before a U.S. Senate committee, the testimony explains the number of countries into which Wyeth markets formula, the functions of professional service representatives, and the development of nonverbal, that is, graphic instructions for formula preparation. ICIFI is also mentioned.

333. Villar, Jose and Jose M. Belizan.
"Breastfeeding in Developing Countries." *Lancet* 8247:621, September 19, 1981.
This important study shows that low-birth-weight infants, fed by undernourished mothers, a common occurrence in less-developed countries, need more than unsupplemented breastfeeding to correct malnutrition. The authors also explain that the milk production of poorly nourished mothers is only 500 to 700 milliliters per day. The needs of infants for the first few months are consistently higher than that average.

334. Walker, A. R. P.
"Infant Feeding Practices in South Africa: An Appraisal of Their Significance to Health." *South African Medical Journal* 54(20):820, November 11, 1978.
This publication concerns itself with the pervasiveness of breastfeeding among whites, coloreds and blacks in South Africa. Breastfeeding is still high among rural and urban blacks, but even here there is some shifting to bottle feeding. The author believes that this leads to increased morbidity and mortality, especially among the lower economic groups.

335. Walker, Isobel.
"Breast or Bottle." *British Medical Journal* 2(6190):609, September 8, 1979.
This letter explains the added difficulties which mothers who are also pursuing professional careers have in breastfeeding their young.

336. Waterlow, J. C.
"Observations on the Protein and Energy Requirements of Pre-School Children." Paper given at the National Institute of Nutrition, Diamond Jubilee, October 1978.
Waterlow's conclusion on the subject of the length of time during which infants can be breastfed without supplementation given certain protein and energy needs, is that infants require supplementation after about two months. He is using Western breast milk production figures to come to that conclusion. He points out that his arguments for early supplementation will apply with even more force to the lower milk outputs of malnourished mothers in less-developed countries.

337. Waterlow, J. C. and A. M. Thomson.
"Observations on the Adequacy of Breast-Feeding." *Lancet* 2:238, August 4, 1979.
After about three months, breastfeeding alone in developing countries may not be providing enough protein and energy to keep the growth of the child from faltering, say these two tropical medicine experts. Supplementation has its own dangers, namely external infections; this, however, can occur due to malnourishment at the breast. Rowland has called this difficult situation the "weanling's dilemma". This is an important article for understanding the complexity of infant health in less-developed countries.

338. Waterlow, J. C.
"Observations on the Suckling's Dilemma — A Personal View." *Journal of Human Nutrition* 35:85, 1981.
The author discusses the subject of early growth in infants in less-developed countries. Growth rates below certain weight standards are related, says the author, to breast milk output and infections. Various results from different countries are presented.

339. Watkinson, M.
"Delayed Onset of Weanling Diarrhoea Associated with High Breast Milk Intake." *Transactions of the Royal Society of Tropical Medicine and Hygiene* 75:432, 1981.
In Keneba, Gambia those infants whose breast milk intake exceeded the group mean were given traditional supplementary foods later than other infants. They weighed on average, after one year, one kilogram more than the other infants, a statistically significant difference.

340. Weinstein, Louis.
"Breast Milk — A Natural Resource." *American Journal of Obstetrics and Gynecology* 136(8):973, April 15, 1980.
The writer urges his fellow obstetricians to take a real interest in encouraging their patients to breastfeed. Breast milk is a natural resource, and physicians should do more to help mothers make use of it for the overall well-being of their infants.

341. Whitehead, R. G.
"Protein-Energy Malnutrition and Breastfeeding." *Nestle Foundation Annual Report* p. 30, 1978.
Infants in Keneba, Gambia grew well for about the first two months of life according to this study. After that, at three and four months, growth falters according to weight-for-age standards. Barring below weight infants and above average production of breast milk, exclusive breastfeeding did not generally satisfy the theoretic energy requirements of infants beyond the first two or three months.

342. Whitehead, R. G., et al.
"Factors Influencing Lactation Performance in Rural Gambian Mothers." *Lancet* ii:178, July 22, 1978.
The authors studied breastfeeding and other feeding practices in a rural African community. Breastfeeding was generally practiced there

until the age of eighteen months. By the sixth month, the weight of these children was falling steadily from international standards. Of course, this is not to say that breast milk was not making an important contribution to the nutrition of the children. The authors also found that the introduction of supplemental cereal feeding did not adversely affect the mothers' milk production in any significant way.

343. Whitehead, R. G.
"Infant Feeding Practices and the Development of Malnutrition in Rural Gambia." *Food and Nutrition Bulletin* 1:36, 1979.
The writer finds that a combination of nutritionally deficient, dangerously contaminated weaning foods and inadequate amounts of breast milk resulted in a gradual fall in percentage weight for age in rural Gambia.

344. Whitehead, R. G.
"Nutrition and Lactation." *The Postgraduate Medical Journal* 55:303, 1979.
Maternal diet has an effect upon breast milk production and the make-up of that breast milk. Dietary intakes in industrial versus less-developed countries is discussed with particular reference to Gambia.

345. Whitehead, R. G. and A. A. Paul.
"Infant Growth and Human Milk Requirements: A Fresh Approach." *Lancet* ii:161, 1981.
The writers say that the breast milk produced by mothers in Western countries is generally higher in volume than that produced by mothers in less-developed countries. The children of this latter group of mothers are generally smaller as well. The authors, using Gambia as a typical less-developed country, explain that average breast milk production for an average-sized infant would be sufficient for between ten and twelve weeks depending upon sex. Their studies indicate that supplementary feeding will be necessary at some stage between four and six months.

346. Woodruff, Calvin W.
"The Science of Infant Nutrition and the Art of Infant Feeding." *Journal of the American Medical Association* 240(7):657, August 1978.
The Committee on Nutrition of the American Academy of Pediatrics issued recommendations which are used by the author to evaluate various forms of infant feeding. Breast milk and infant formulas meet the requirements of these recommendations while evaporated milk, cow's milk and skimmed milk do not. Other nutrients, such as strained foods and infant cereals, should be given when the infant has developed the ability to take food from a spoon, somewhere between three and six months.

347. World Health Organization.
Annotated Agenda, "Meeting on Infant and Young Child Feeding". Geneva: WHO/UNICEF, October 9-12, 1979.
The six-page agenda proposes a host of "themes for discussion" at the "Meeting on Infant and Young Child Feeding". Suggested topics include the role that governments ought to play in following up the

recommendations of the meeting, the consideration of whether an international code of conduct and ethics was needed to limit the marketing of infant formula, and many other themes. Also of interest is the list of governments and non-governmental organizations (NGOs) participating in the meeting. Well represented among the NGOs are most of the groups opposing the international formula manufacturers.

348. World Health Organization.
Background Paper, "Meeting on Infant and Young Child Feeding". Geneva: WHO/UNICEF, October 9-12, 1979.
This lengthy document is divided into two major parts. Part I summarizes certain knowledge about infant and young child feeding. By its own statement, it does not aim at being "comprehensive". Part II presents relevant themes for discussion at the meeting as seen by WHO/UNICEF. Part I of the paper is low-key and balanced. Part II is more partisan in that many of the suggested discussion topics are unfavorably formulated towards infant formula manufacturers. Their products are described as inappropriate and the demand for them is referred to as "unnecessary". Industrially prepared weaning foods are called convenience foods rather than foods of necessity. Company distribution of commercial products is called unjustified, and the use of governmentally enforced codes is favored. The two parts are quite different in tone and content.

349. World Health Organization.
Recommendations, Appropriate Marketing and Distribution of Infant Formula and Weaning Foods, "Meeting on Infant and Young Child Feeding". Geneva: WHO/UNICEF, October 9-12, 1979.
Ten paragraphs of recommendations were produced by the meeting. The most important recommendation was the agreement to hold further sessions to design an international code of marketing of infant formula products. The recommendations also endorse breastfeeding as the best way for infants to be fed. Promotion of breast milk substitutes to the general public was prohibited by one of the paragraphs. The ultimate responsibility for a food and nutrition policy was said to reside in the government of each country. The recommendations seem to allow the promotion of formula directly to physicians and health workers. Nestle, it should be noted, endorsed the recommendations.

350. World Health Organization.
"World Health Organization Collaborative Study on Breastfeeding: Methods and Main Results of the Study — Preliminary Report." Geneva: WHO, MCH/79.3, 1979.
This lengthy and often referred to study contains a wealth of helpful information about breastfeeding and formula use in less-developed countries. On the whole it tends to show that mothers in the Third World continue to breastfeed for the early months of their child's life. The study also contains data about the effects of hospital stays on breastfeeding as well as numerous charts and graphs which adeptly display the evidence they are intended to illustrate. Much insight can be gained into the variety and universality of feeding practices based upon this study of 23,000 women in nine countries.

351. World Health Organization.
"Infant and Young Child Feeding: Draft International Code of Marketing of Breast-Milk Substitutes — Report by the Director General." WHO, 67th Session, Provisional Agenda Item 20.2, EB67/20, December 10, 1980.
This is a draft of the Code which contains a description of the process of development used to create the draft. The draft is presented in two forms, one being in the form of a "regulation" and the other in the form of a "recommendation". It was in the latter form that the Code was adopted May 1981.

352. World Health Organization.
Contemporary Patterns of Breastfeeding: Report of the WHO Collaborative Study on Breastfeeding. Geneva: World Health Organization, 1981.
This report recounts the results of surveys of breastfeeding practices in selected countries. It includes 55 pages of charts, graphs and interview forms. Like other social science studies, it reaches ambivalent conclusions, in this case, about the prevalence of breastfeeding, lactation and fertility, health services and the like.

353. World Health Organization.
"Resolution of the 34th World Health Assembly." International Code of Marketing of Breastmilk Substitutes, Fifteenth Plenary Meeting, 21 May 1981. *Nutrition Today* p. 13, July/August 1981.
This is the WHO International Code of Marketing of Breastmilk Substitutes adopted after discussion May 21, 1981. After a lengthy preamble, the Code prohibits advertising of infant formula to the general public, allows but limits the provision of marketing information to health professionals, and requires labeling which: (1) claims that breastfeeding is superior to formula feeding, (2) states that the product should be used only with the advice of health workers, and (3) gives appropriate instructions for safe preparation.

354. World Health Organization.
"The World Health Organization Code of Marketing of Breastmilk Substitutes." Statement by Board of Directors of the Ambulatory Pediatric Association. *Pediatrics* 68(3):432, September 1981.
The Ambulatory Pediatrics Association urged the United States delegation to the World Health Assembly to vote for the WHO Code governing the marketing of infant formula. This statement strongly protests the United States vote against the Code and presents its reasons.

355. Wray, J. D.
"Maternal Nutrition, Breastfeeding and Infant Survival," In: Mosley, W. H., ed. Nutrition and Human Reproduction. New York: Plenum Press, 1978; p. 197.
The author shows the relationship between maternal nutrition and lactation. There is a certain minimum diet below which lactation quality and quantity will be affected adversely. Dr. Wray reviews infant mortality data from the West over the last 100 years and shows that they picture a steady decline in mortality among all infants, breastfed and artificially fed. Until recently the mortality among artificially fed infants was higher than among those who were breastfed. That difference is attributed to the poor quality of the

substitute feeds. Data is also analyzed from Latin America and the Caribbean.

356. Zeitlin, M., et al.
"Breastfeeding and Nutritional Status in Depressed Urban Areas of Greater Manila, Philippines." *Ecology of Food and Nutrition* 7:103, 1978.
The most important factors in determining the nutritional status of the children who were the subject of this study in Manila, the Philippines were socio-economic conditions, birth order, education of the mother and morbidity. Bottle feeding or length of breastfeeding were not statistically significant causes of malnutrition in the over 500 cases studied.

C. NEWS ARTICLES

357. Abrams, Elliott.
"Infant Formula Code: Why the U.S. May Stand Alone." *Washington Post* May 21, 1981.
This editorial discusses why the United States voted against the World Health Organization's International Code of Marketing of Breastmilk Substitutes. The U.S. vote occurred shortly after the May 1981 adoption of the Code in "recommendation" form by WHO.

358. Aho, Colleen.
"A Code for Infant Foods Marketing?" *Interfocus* (The Minnesota Daily), September 22, 1980.
This is a fairly objective look at the controversy from the perspective of a university student.

359. Anderson, Kurt.
"The Battle of the Bottle." *Time* p. 26, June 1, 1981.
This news report comments on the failure of the Reagan administration to support the WHO Code when many other countries favored its adoption.

360. "The Baby Formula Controversy."
The Daily Pennsylvanian (University of Pennsylvania), October 23, 1981.
Neal Bluher, a member of the Pennsylvania Consumer Board, replies to those who had earlier called for a boycott of Nestle products. The opinion editorial emphasizes that the debate over formula feeding is one between two valid positions. Nestle is guided by the profit motive and INFACT (Infant Formula Action Coalition) is guided by anti-business sentiments. There are no new sources cited here, but the arguments are well and concisely made.

361. "Baby Milk Boycott."
Nursing Mirror 151(5):14, July 31, 1980.
The London-based Baby Milk Action Coalition is the subject of this brief news article. The announcement says that BMAC is launching the Nestle boycott to protest the sale of formula to the Third World.

362. Barness, Lewis A.
"Formula Manufacture and Infant Feeding." Editorial, *Journal of the American Medical Association* 243(10):1075, March 14, 1980.
The author gives a balanced view of infant formula manufacturers.

On one hand, they should not be castigated. They have produced helpful and healthful products. On the other hand, they sometimes err as in cases where deficiencies in formulas caused reactions in infants. Producing formula which is as close to mother's milk as possible, for those who cannot breastfeed, ought to be the goal of pediatricians and industry policy.

363. Barovick, Richard L.
"International." *Public Relations Journal* 35(11):2, November 1979.
This is an announcement of the 1979 WHO meeting in Geneva and a listing of the various protagonists.

364. "Battling the Baby Bottle."
Wall Street Journal p. 24, May 4, 1981.
In this editorial the writer calls the WHO Infant Formula Marketing Code foolish and insidious because it is advocated on the basis of little evidence. With a note of irony the editorialist comments that the oral rehydration of infants by WHO/UNICEF in which a salt-sugar formula must often be given with unclean water is not condemned whereas Nestle is held to a higher standard as it distributes formula. The comparison between oral rehydration and formula feeding is not altogether a fair one, but there are similarities.

365. "Beaten With a Baby Bottle."
Wall Street Journal p. 32, June 9, 1981.
This editorial states that Dr. Ernest Lefever was unfairly treated during congressional confirmation hearings because of his organization's receipt of Nestle funds.

366. Beck, Joan.
"Showdown on Infant Formulas." *The Chicago Tribune* May 1, 1981.
Approaching the dispute over formula feeding from a new angle, the writer of this opinion editorial favors some supervision by international bodies of the marketing of infant formula, but is opposed to the proposed WHO Code since it interferes with the Third World mother's right to decide to breastfeed or not. Women should have a free and informed choice as to whether or not they will breastfeed their babies.

367. "A Boycott over Infant Formula: Nestle Co."
Business Week p. 137, April 23, 1979.
A short article in the earlier part of the controversy, this piece contains accurate reporting, although very little scientific evidence is offered to explain the complex issues to which reference is made.

368. Brooke, Jim.
"Criticism Mounts Over Use of Baby Formulas Among World's Poor — Brazil Promotes Breastfeeding." *Washington Post* April 21, 1981.
This news story reports on the Brazilian government's campaign to encourage breastfeeding within its borders by means of posters, television and radio spots, and other means in urban and rural areas.

369. Bruning, Fred, et al.
"Infant Feeding: Breast Is Best." *Newsweek* October 22, 1979.
This is a short article which fairly presents the views of both sides of

the dispute early in the controversy. The general conclusion reached is that Third World mothers may prefer breastfeeding, but they often choose, for a variety of reasons, to engage in formula feeding.

370. "Campus Crunch: Boycott of Nestle Products over Controversial Baby Formula." *Newsweek* 92:115, November 27, 1978.
Appearing in the "Education" section of this national publication, the article tells of various student groups on American campuses which are pressing their food services to boycott Nestle products and urging their fellow classmates to stop consuming Nestle confections and other products. Some of the campuses mentioned are Wellesley, Yale, Colgate, Providence and the University of Minnesota.

371. Chavez, Lydia.
"Baby Formula Makers Unfazed: Concerns Say New Curb Is Innocuous." *New York Times* p. D1, May 22, 1981.
This is a report concerning the adoption of the WHO Code which quotes infant formula firm officials as saying that they are not opposed to the Code as passed. They also emphasize that the Code is voluntary so that individual nations will have to choose whether or not to adopt it.

372. "Code's Adoption Closes Chapter in Bettering of Infant, Child Health." *World Health* p. 30, August 1981.
The adoption of the WHO Code by the World Health Assembly is the subject of this brief news item which quotes reactions from newspapers in London, India, New York and Washington.

373. "Codes of Conduct: Worry Over New Restraints on Multinationals." *Chemical Week* July 15, 1981.
This unsigned report focuses on the implications of codes of conduct for firms doing business as multinationals, arguing further that such codes may well change the way firms conduct themselves for better or for worse.

374. "Controversial Code for Mother's Milk." *Science News* 119:340, May 30, 1981.
This item notes the adoption of the WHO Code and its possible effects in the United States.

375. Culbert, Mike.
"Infant Formula, A Capitalist Plot." *Tri-Valley Herald* (CA) p. 14, Sunday, August 17, 1980.
In this syndicated column, the Nestle controversy is reviewed, stressing that it has scientific and political dimensions, and criticizing the activists who link it to radical social, anti-capitalist views.

376. Docksai, M. Fisk.
"Infant Formula Standards Set." *Trial* 16:16, November 1980.
This short news item does not deal directly with the Nestle controversy, but indicates that if formula producers in the United States fail to produce a safe formula product, product liability suits may be filed by the families of infants who have consumed the inadequate formula.

The article refers to the exclusion of salt from a certain formula in the United States.

377. Downing, John.
"Why Boycott Nestle?" *Toronto Sun* (Ontario), October 28, 1981.
In this discussion of attempts by critic groups to get the Toronto Board of Health to support the Nestle boycott, an alderman was quoted as saying that Nestle was guilty until proven innocent, a proposal with which the writer of the article vehemently disagreed. Downing challenges the lack of knowledge of the Board concerning Third World countries and maintains that there is no obvious evidence that Nestle "kills babies".

378. "Facts About the Most National of Multinationals."
Interfocus (Minnesota Daily), September 22, 1980.
This brief item in a student newspaper portrays Nestle solely as made up of greedy capitalists and exploitive monopolists.

379. Foran, D.
"Infant Formula in Kenya: Promotion by Nestle." *America* 139:497, December 30, 1978.
This short account is based upon an individual's visit to Kenya in which he observed and recorded the use of infant formula which was common. Some of the conclusions seem to be exaggerations — such as "formula is sold in every food store in the country". The author does point out that for many families, infant formula is simply too expensive, and that mothers can "rarely afford it". The piece, however, still blames the infant formula, by implication, for the bulk of disease and malnutrition among Kenya's infants. Nestle's response is characterized as a public relations response and Foran labels the dispute "the baby formula scandal".

380. Geddes, John M.
"Nestle Seeking Market Balance: Increased Sales in Third World Pose Problems." *New York Times* p. D1, March 27, 1980.
Recounted here are the business challenges of the 1970s for Nestle and ways the firm hopes to avoid these problems in the 1980s. The boycott issue is mentioned.

381. Gephardt, Thomas.
"Wisdom of Serpents Is Missing in Crusades." *Cincinnati Enquirer* Section 1, July 13, 1980.
This is a general commentary about the tactics of people involved in social crusades, the Nestle affair being one briefly mentioned.

382. Gephardt, Thomas.
"The Debate Continues About Infant Formula." *Cincinnati Enquirer* June 28, 1981.
In this brief newspaper column, the stages of the formula controversy are set out. Noted particularly are false assumptions about the problem.

383. Gilliam, Dorothy.
"Nestle Boycott: No Profit in Sick Babies." *Washington Post* Monday, June 1, 1981.
This is a brief, highly opinionated article, hostile to Nestle, and lacking substantial facts.

384. Goessl, Joan.
"Speaker Says Formula Harms Third World Babies." *Milwaukee Journal* September 19, 1979.
This news item recounts the public arguments of Doug Johnson on the Nestle controversy. Johnson opposes Nestle's promotional activities in the less-developed world and heads the Infant Formula Action Coalition, INFACT.

385. Grant, James.
"Nestle Crunch: The Campaign Against Infant Formula Reeks of Sophistry." *Barron's* p. 7, July 16, 1979.
This is an editorial criticizing the weak arguments of the Nestle boycott proponents. Special attention is given to Senate testimony before Senator Edward Kennedy.

386. Guest, I.
"Ban Adopted on Advertising Baby Foods." *International Herald Tribune* October 13-14, 1979.
This news item notes changes in the way international firms advertise formula in Third World nations.

387. Guthrie, George M.
"W.H.O. Infant Formula Code Misses Real Problem." Editorial, *The Herald* (Sharon, PA), p. 4, Saturday, May 30, 1981.
This opinion editorial by a psychologist and nutritionist argues that breast milk production by many Third World mothers is adequate in quality but insufficient in quantity. He believes that formula can be misused but that the WHO Code is harmful because it diverts attention from more fundamental issues such as the improvement of sanitary conditions and the need for maternal supplements.

388. "Harvard President Rebuffs Pleas by Activists to Support Boycotts."
New York Times p. B7, May 21, 1979.
This unsigned news item reports President Derek Bok's decision to ignore student demands that Harvard support the boycott against Nestle.

389. Hempstone, Smith.
"All This Breast-Beating About Infant Formula." *The Washington Star* July 8, 1981.
This is a sympathetic account of the United States refusal to support the WHO Code.

390. "In Dubious Bottle."
Commonweal 108:325, June 5, 1981.
This article reports the failure of the United States to support the international code devised by WHO for the marketing of infant formula, and views this failure as an embarrassment.

391. "Indian Premier Says Drug Firms Are Profiteering."
Wall Street Journal p. 31, May 7, 1981.
This is a report of Indira Gandhi's observations on the formula manufacturers.

392. "The Infant Food Industry."
Lancet 1(8076):1240, June 10, 1978.
Stating that they had earlier criticized the infant food industry, the commentators now point out that they are glad to see that the industry is cooperating with efforts to study and deal with certain problems without the "wounding exchanges" which had seemed to dominate previous discussions.

393. "Infant-Formula Boycott an Unreasonable Action."
Durham Morning Herald (N.C.) October 20, 1981.
This editorial opposes the boycott and asks readers to resist the efforts of some to brand formula companies as baby killers. Apparently, a grocery store in the locale had complied with boycotter's demands to cancel its direct account with Nestle and had handed out bags with the boycott message printed on it. The editorial opposes that kind of action because it deprives other consumers of choice. This editorial shows how an international issue was translated into a local concern.

394. "Infant Formula Controversy Has Two Sides."
Michigan Christian Advocate (Adrian, MI) March 12, 1981.
This news article about the infant feeding debate refers to many of the principal parties including Dr. Michael Latham, Dr. Philip Wogaman and others. The developments leading up to the consideration of the WHO Code are reviewed.

395. "Infant Formula: How Safe?"
Consumers Research Magazine 64:4, August 1981.
Apparently in response to inquiries about whether infant formula was safe for use in the United States, this brief summary was put out to readers of *Consumers Research Magazine* emphasizing that it is not formula itself which is inherently dangerous, but the unclean water and the unsanitary preparation of the formula which present problems to users in various parts of world. The writer also points out that the absence of formula in less-developed countries will not end the misery that results from the use of unclean water to prepare native weaning foods.

396. Ioannou, Lori.
"WHO Study 'Contradicts' Its Infant Formula Code." *NY Journal of Commerce* July 10, 1981.
The author of this news item quotes statements by Bristol-Myers in which they point out that formula advertising is not given as a reason mothers bottle feed instead of breastfeed. It is claimed that the U.N. Collaborative Study on Breastfeeding does not support the need for the Code.

397. Keller, H. Anton.
"Behind WHO's Ban on Baby Formula Ads." *Wall Street Journal* 197:20, June 29, 1981.
This article argues that the formula industry's strategy for dealing with issues at the WHO Code meeting was not well-conceived.

398. "Killer in a Bottle."
Economist 279:50, May 9-15, 1981.
This unsigned article states that because of restrictions on baby bottle sales, baby formula can be obtained only by prescription in Papua, New Guinea. The article continues with a discussion of the WHO meeting in progress in Geneva.

399. Lefever, Ernest.
"Crunch Over Nestle Called Unfounded." *Wall Street Journal* p. 13, August 24, 1981.
In this letter from Dr. Ernest Lefever to *Wall Street Journal,* he defends himself against charges that the receipt by his Ethics and Public Policy Center of a contribution from Nestle Company was improper because the Center had reprinted an article opposing the boycott of Nestle products.

400. Lusinchi, Victor.
"Baby-Food Industry Agrees to a Curb on the Promotion of Infant Formulas." *New York Times* Saturday, October 13, 1979.
This is a discussion of the industry's agreement to abide by the WHO recommendations produced in 1979.

401. Mathews, T., et al.
"Breast vs. the Bottle." *Newsweek* 97:54, June 1, 1981.
This news item comments on the Reagan administration's failure to support the passage of the WHO Code.

402. "Motherhood, Too."
New Republic 184:8, May 30, 1981.
This is an unsigned article dealing with the failure of President Reagan's administration to support the WHO Code.

403. "Mother's Milk."
America 144:456, June 6, 1981.
This editorial opposes the United States government's position against the WHO Code.

404. "Mother's Milk."
Scientific American 245:68, August 1981.
This unsigned article refers to the failure of the Reagan administration to support the WHO Code and then proceeds with a technical discussion of the differences between natural milk and formulas.

405. "The Nestle Boycott Kills Babies."
Wall Street Journal p. 28, November 1, 1979.
This editorial evaluates the INFACT charges against Nestle in the context of the history of the dispute and finds that the charges do not

hold up. Formula companies have been almost too willing to accommodate their critics.

406. "News Formula."
National Review 33:942, August 21, 1981.
The position of this short commentary is that over the past decade international agencies have changed from being supporters of formula distribution as a supplement to opponents of formula usage. The writer is referring to the recently enacted WHO Code. The only alternative to formula supplements after the early months of life is native weaning foods which are dangerous and less nutritious than commercial products, argues the writer.

407. "Peace Overture From Nestle."
Christian Century p. 1049, October 21, 1981.
This brief item points to a meeting between Nestle officials and the United Methodist Infant Formula Task Force to exchange views on various infant feeding issues.

408. Raphael, Dana.
"Nestle Boycott." *Journal of Nurse-Midwifery* 26(1):39, January/February 1981.
This is a letter response to earlier comments by Doug Johnson. Raphael has a way of cutting through pretense and of righting imbalance, explaining that though activist groups complained about the lobbying of Nestle at the various WHO conferences, delegates complained that other non-governmental groups had engaged in aggressive lobbying. Raphael is concerned that pressure groups will be more likely to influence the decisions of world health bodies than scientific evidence.

409. Solender, Elsa A.
"Woman Watch — Infant Formula Furor." *Jewish Times* (Baltimore, MD) May 29, 1981.
This writer distrusts the hyperbole of the infant formula activists and is doubtful that the U.N. is the correct international agency to which to entrust the making of a regulatory code. The editorial favors the printing of warnings to mothers on formula tins so that misuse can be reduced. The piece asks why boycott campaigners have not spent more time on improving general health conditions rather than opposing Nestle.

410. Solomon, S.
"Controversy Over Infant Formula." *New York Times Magazine* p. 92, December 6, 1981.
The complete list of questions raised by the formula feeding debate is touched upon by this relatively brief article. The distinction between bottle feeding and formula feeding is mentioned as well as the central problem of suitable weaning foods. The article does not reach a single conclusion, but on the whole it grasps the subtlety of the questions which make up the dispute.

411. Sutton, Barbara.
"Scientist Says Nestle Is Changing Practices." *The Daily Orange* (S.U.N.Y.), October 19, 1981.
The appearance of Nestle representative Neils Christiansen is reported

in this news article. He stressed the compliance of Nestle's current practices with the WHO Code. Questions were put to him on sampling and on the subject of preparation of the formula with contaminated water.

412. Thornton, J. and A. Zanker.
"U.S. Vote on Baby Formula that Stirred a Storm" *U.S. News* 90:60, June 1, 1981.
This item comments on the decision of the Reagan administration not to support the WHO Code.

413. Tyrrell, R. Emmett.
"Formula for Meddling." *Washington Post* Monday, May 25, 1981.
This editorial opinion item opposes the sweeping nature of the WHO Code and supports United States opposition to it. In some places in the world, if improperly prepared, formula may be a menace, but in other parts of the world it is a real blessing. The U.N. should not intrude itself into the realm of free choice. That function is well beyond its mandate.

414. Wasserman, Ursula.
"WHO: Breast Is Best." 14 *Journal of World Trade Law* 451, September/October 1980.
This article explains developments that led toward the passage of the WHO Code regulating formula marketing. Wasserman also refers to the British medical journal, *The Lancet,* and its view that, though there is evidence that a decrease in breastfeeding, where it has occurred, has been harmful, nevertheless, extensive malnutrition and disease have not been solely due to milk substitutes.

415. Webbe, Stephen.
"The Nestle Boycott: Is It Fair?" *Christian Science Monitor* p. B11, July 31, 1979.
This article summarizes the position of INFACT and infant formula producer Nestle S.A. while asking questions about the ethics of the Nestle boycott.

416. "WHO Drafts A Marketing Code."
World Business Weekly p. 8, January 19, 1981.
The article reports the development of the WHO Code which at the time of the article was in draft form and was being considered by the various parties that stood to be affected by it. The formula industry group, ICIFI, and the international coalition of boycott supporters, IBFAN, are both referred to by the writer.

417. Wild, William H.
"WHO's Big Lie Formula Exposed." *The Journal-Herald* (Dayton, OH), Saturday, December 5, 1981.
This editorial takes a strong stand against the WHO Code based on the WHO studies on breastfeeding patterns in the Third World. The writer also refers to the work of *Reason* magazine writer James Hickel. He challenges the readers to look at the facts and refuse to join the boycott.

418. "Work Within Our Walls."
UVA Daily (University of Virginia - Charlottesville, VA) November 20, 1981.
Student interest in the Nestle boycott was often keen, but by no means did students always end up on the same side of the question, as shown by this editorial in the *University of Virginia Daily*. The writer here questions the boycott because it is being proposed by a campus group whose motives he questions. Are they really interested in the health of Third World infants, or are they distraught over large corporations and intent upon seeing that somehow and in some way they are discredited?

D. CRITIC GROUPS

419. Allain, Jean-Pierre.
"Bottle Feeding: A Symbol of Progress?" Reprint, Minneapolis: International Baby Food Action Network, March 1981.
This piece by those opposing infant formula marketing in less-developed countries is a sketchy review of the controversy involving Nestle. Nestle and other manufacturers are over-promoting and unconcerned with the harm they are allegedly doing. Company dividends are said to be preferred over the lives and health of innocent children.

420. "Baby Food Politics."
ISIS International Bulletin ISIS Collective, 7:17, Spring 1978.
A single general theme comes through this short and sometimes strident article: Transnational corporations are exploiting women and their children for profit. These firms, large and international, are in league with governments and health care professionals of the less-developed world. The other materials to which the reader is referred by a short bibliography are on only one side of the question.

421. "Battle of the Bottle: The Babyfood Companies vs. Asia's Children."
Asiaweek June 19, 1981. (Reprinted by International Baby Food Action Network.)
This article maintains that international infant formula manufacturers gave "howls of rage" when the WHO Code was recently approved. That tone pervades the piece and makes it into an account of the controversy which ignores the complex realities of infant feeding. The article concentrates on Malaysia, Singapore and the Philippines for its examples. It describes various codes of ethics and marketing in place or being proposed to control infant formula sales in Asia.

422. Brown, E.
"Boycott Works — It Better." *Humanist* 40:50, January/February 1980.
This article champions the work of the World Health Organization as it conducted meetings in late 1979. The author refers to her children and how they helped join in the boycott of Nestle products. The article adds litte to the dispute, but it shows the depth of feeling and support which was mustered among various groups for the boycott.

423. Chetley, Andy.
"Marketing Breast Milk Substitutes." *Lancet* August 2, 1980.
This letter to the editor contains statements and charges by Mr. Chetley, an opponent of Nestle, regarding an earlier letter which appeared in *The Lancet*. Chetley refers to the pressure brought by multinationals to dilute the WHO efforts at making a restrictive code that would govern formula sales in the less-developed world.

424. Clarkson, Fred.
"The Cost of Promotion." Minneapolis: INFACT, no date.
This essay pamphlet, reprinted from *Sojourners* (no date given), argues that the infant formula problem is as much a problem in the United States as it is in the Third World. A similar argument has been made by other groups without much success.

425. Clement, Douglas.
"Infant Formula Malnutrition Threat to the Third World." *Christian Century* 95:208, March 1, 1978; Discussion 95:708, July 19, 1978.
The author of this piece is an INFACT official who presents the classic case of the INFACT argument, stating categorically that use of formula in Third World countries has brought about malnutrition and disease. Following the article is a letter supporting the Clement position by Jean Richardson.

426. Clement, Douglas.
"Nestle's Latest Killing in the Bottle Baby Market." *Business and Society Review* 26:60, 1978.
This article charges Nestle with continuing to produce contaminated formula for sale in Australia after it discovered that its equipment contained salmonella bacteria. Clement also refers to a similar case in Colombia and then brings in the sale of formula in less-developed countries.

427. Cramer-Heuerman, J. and G. M. Willems.
"To End the Infant Formula Tragedy: The Boycott of Nestle." *Engage/Social Action* 7:26, 1979.
The authors review how the Nestle boycott commenced and characterize Nestle's continuing sales to less-developed countries as the result of aggressive promotional activities. The demands of INFACT are listed, and it is said by the writers, both of INFACT, that Nestle has failed to significantly change its marketing practices in response to those demands. Mentioned also is a bill introduced to Congress May 1979 to regulate infant formula sales. It did not pass.

428. Hoskin, Fran P.
"The Politics of Breastfeeding." *Women's International Network News* Summer 1981.
The point of this essay is captured in the sentence which states that the WHO Code was adopted by a male-run commission. Women are left out of the decision-making process in this controversy, it notes.

429. Infant Formula Action Coalition.
UPDATE. Minneapolis: INFACT.
This is one of the official publications of INFACT, one of the most

vociferous groups leading the attack on Nestle. All these *UPDATES* are critical of Nestle, often in strident, caustic terms. The repetitive nature of these numerous *UPDATES* prevents exhaustive listing in this bibliography, even though a few particular issues have been included.

430. Infant Formula Action Coalition.
"The Nestle Boycott." Minneapolis: INFACT, December 1978.
Doug Johnson, National Chairman of INFACT, writes an impassioned form letter, exhorting members of the American public to save the lives of millions of Third World babies by giving money to INFACT and boycotting Nestle. This letter is representative of the type and quality of material mass produced by INFACT.

431. Infant Formula Action Coalition.
"Nestlegate." Minneapolis: Haymarket Press, Fall 1980.
Distributed by ICCR and INFACT, this pamphlet is an exposition of a memo, questionably obtained, in which Nestle executives discuss their strategy for dealing with the boycott. The use of public relations consultants and a strategy of trying to encourage third parties to write favorable articles is what the writers see here as ominous.

432. "Infant Formula and Exploitation."
The Intellectual Activist June 1, 1981.
This publication features the infant formula dispute. Basically, it questions the effects of government regulation of the feeding choices of mothers in the Third World. The article points out that infant formula may be very important to the malnourished mother.

433. Interfaith Center on Corporate Responsibility.
Briefs. NY: ICCR.
These *"Briefs"* are included in each edition of ICCR's *Corporate Examiner* and highlight a particular social area, usually focusing on one or more corporations. Several examples are cited throughout this bibliography, but the number of those dealing specifically with Nestle are too numerous and too repetitive to be exhaustively included. The tone of the *"Briefs"* is generally hostile toward big business and multinational enterprises.

434. Interfaith Center on Corporate Responsibility.
The Corporate Examiner. NY: ICCR.
This publication is regularly put out by the Interfaith Center on Corporate Responsibility, and each issue deals with some pertinent conflict between corporate behavior and social ethics. Numerous issues involved the Nestle controversy specifically and some of the more important ones are cited throughout this bibliography. The publication is essentially hostile towards multinational corporations and inflammatory language is often employed when criticizing "capitalist exploitation".

435. Interfaith Center on Corporate Responsibility.
Letter and information packet to delegates for 1980 meeting on Infant and Young Child Feeding. NY: ICCR, April 17, 1980.
Leaders of the boycott campaign urge delegates at one of many world

health conferences having to do with infant feeding to vote in favor of the efforts to develop a code of formula feeding and promotion. Attached to the letter are various items which favor the boycotter's position, such as a short article by Anil Agarwil on "The Milk that Kills", a report from a portion of *The Lancet* on the WHO/UNICEF meeting, and an editorial from the *Corporate Examiner* as to "Why the Nestle Boycott Must Continue".

436. Interfaith Center on Corporate Responsibility.
"The 'Code of Marketing of Breastmilk Substitutes' Is Born." NY: ICCR, September 1981.
The ICCR issued this introduction to the WHO Code, which was passed in May 1981. The introduction is replete with ICCR's views that the Code was needed to prevent commerciogenic malnutrition from leading to the death of millions of infants in the Third World. The exceedingly suspicious tone of the work sometimes does harm to the issues raised, as when Abbott/Ross' donation of architectural services to hospitals is seen as a way by which they can separate mothers from infants and thus encourage the use of formula. The infant formula industry is described as thoroughly discredited by their actions in connection with the World Health Assembly. A shortened version of the WHO Code is presented as well.

437. Interfaith Center on Corporate Responsibility.
"Study By Public Interest Law Firm Charges Baby Formula Use Is Also a U.S. Problem." *The Corporate Examiner* 10(8-9), September 1981.
In June 1981, a public interest law firm in San Francisco presented a petition to various governmental agencies which alleged that the sale and distribution of infant formula in the United States was a health and nutrition problem. According to the petition, which is reported in this publication, non-English-speaking and illiterate mothers are said to be among the heaviest users of the formula.

438. International Baby Food Action Network.
Newsletter. Minneapolis: IBFAN.
The IBFAN News is a monthly publication with in-depth coverage of what is happening internationally with the boycott and recent alleged company violations.

439. International Baby Food Action Network.
"Infant Formula Promotion, 1980." Minneapolis: IBFAN, 1980.
IBFAN, supported by the groups opposed to formula marketing practices in Third World countries, issued regular reports of alleged violations of public commitments against formula feeding promotion made by major manufacturers. No WHO Code existed at the time of this report although later reports were geared to reporting non-compliance with the WHO Code. Most of the incidents reported involved posters, sampling, or other kinds of promotional efforts. The reporting is not very specific, which is to say that the researcher would have trouble verifying the complaints with the information presented.

440. International Baby Food Action Network.
"Infant Formula Promotion, 1981." Minneapolis: IBFAN, May 1981.
This is the May 1981 report of IBFAN, a network of groups opposed to

the formula marketing practices of multinational companies in Third World countries. Later reports refer to specific violations of the WHO Code, but this report is the last one which simply reports certain promotional efforts by Nestle and many other companies which are said to occur in spite of representations by the companies that they have ceased all such promotion. The types of violations referred to are the distribution of booklets, posters and other promotional activities which are said to illustrate that words are not being followed by actions. The documentation of the complaints is scanty and the researcher will have difficulty verifying the allegations.

441. Johnson, Douglas.
"A Glimpse at Nestle's Anti-Boycott Strategy." *Business and Sociology Review* 37:65, Spring 1981.
Douglas Johnson writes here about one of the many incidents which occurred during the formula dispute. The article makes accusations about the funds received by a Washington public policy organization since that organization, the Ethics and Public Policy Center, republished an article which had appeared in *Fortune* and which was critical of various groups which had campaigned against the firm's strategy in the controversy. The incident undoubtedly gave some fuel to the boycott fire, but it now seems to be less important than certain other enduring questions.

442. Johnson, Douglas.
Letter, *Third World Institute.* Minneapolis: INFACT, July 10, 1978.
This lengthy letter was written in response to Professor Bwibo's letter of April 14, 1978 in an attempt to discredit Bwibo's caustic attack on Peter Krieg's film "Bottle Babies." Johnson goes through ten pages of detail to support his claim that Bwibo was exploited and manipulated by Nestle, in effect compelling him to write his letter. Johnson's attack on Bwibo eventually dissipates into another attack on Nestle for employing political, economic and social pressure, false, misleading and non-objective information, gifts, and even bribery to secure the support of the influential Dr. Bwibo, and other physicians and health professionals.

443. Johnson, Douglas and Sally Austin Tom.
"Nestle Boycott." *Journal of Nurse-Midwifery* 25(5):4, September/October 1980.
Mr. Johnson, the National Chairman of INFACT, replies to an earlier article in this letter to the editor. He quotes a market survey showing high profits for Nestle in infant formula and mentions UNICEF and U.N. sources on the subject of increased morbidity and mortality from bottle feeding.

444. Kazis, Richard.
"Hot Chocolate." *New Internationalist* No. 67, Summer 1978.
The writers of this article are quick to refer to Nestle as callous and as engaged in the deliberate sacrifice of the health and lives of Third World infants. The dispute is outlined briefly, but most of the article is spent referring to the actions of the Interfaith Center on Corporate Responsibility and INFACT.

445. Margulies, Leah.
"Celebrating the WHO/UNICEF Infant Formula Marketing Code as a 'Minimum Requirement'." Excerpted testimony before Subcommittees of the Foreign Affairs Committee, U.S. House of Representatives, June 16, 1981. Minneapolis: INFACT 1981.
This pamphlet is a printed version, distributed by INFACT, of the testimony given by Ms. Margulies before a committee of the U.S. House in 1981. In it she discusses her views of the Nestle opposition to the WHO Code. She charges Nestle with engaging in "dirty tricks" during the WHO Assembly, although "reliable sources" are the references which she gives for many of these allegations. She does not believe that Nestle will abide by the Code.

446. Peerman, D.
"Conscience of Linda Kelsey." *Christian Century* 97:244, March 5, 1980.
Linda Kelsey, of the "Lou Grant" TV show, says she regrets making a commercial for the Nestle firm three years before, since she now knows the "true" story about Nestle.

447. Post, James E. and Edward Baer.
"Demarketing Infant Formula: Consumer Products in the Developing World." *Journal of Contemporary Business* 7:17, 1979.
The authors view the sale of infant formula in Third World countries as increasing the risks to infants' health, safety and welfare. They point out the complexity of the movement, in some areas, of mothers to formula feeding and away from breastfeeding. They urge the "demarketing" of infant formula by which they mean the elimination of promotion to customers who, they say, will surely misuse the product. Increases in sales volume and improvement in profitability may not be able to be realized under such demarketing, say the authors. The writers do not believe that the industry can police itself in this regard. Instead, there must be constant pressure by critics, international organizations and governments to bring about true demarketing.

448. Ratner, Jonathan.
"Influence-Peddling Nestle Style." *Multinational Monitor* February 1981, p. 6.
This article charges that Nestle has adopted a new strategy to deal with the issues in the formula controversy. That strategy is to "encourage" third parties to address the issues, but to keep a low profile for itself. The writer refers to internal Nestle memos which purport to show the carrying out of such an approach. Nestle support for the Ethics and Public Policy Center is repeatedly mentioned. In terms of balance, the article does not seem to regard boycott efforts to enlist the support of third party groups as falling under the same condemnation.

449. Swiss Action Group for International Development.
Business as Usual. Berne: Third World Action Group, November 1978.
This packet of information includes materials and analysis favoring the Nestle boycott and opposing Nestle. The materials restate the accusation that Nestle is responsible for the deaths of thousands of babies. The materials maintain that Nestle continues to promote its products in unethical ways and describes the development of the

United States boycott, the Senate hearings conducted by Senator Edward Kennedy, and various allegations of aggressive promotion of infant formula in Malaysia, Philippines, Dominican Republic and Guatemala, among others.

450. Tafler, Sue and Betsy Walker.
"Why Boycott Nestle?" *Science for the People* 10:33, January/February 1978. In the article the authors call themselves radicals who wish to educate people in general about the dangers of multinational corporations. The writers seem to argue with themselves about whether a limited objective, like joining in the Nestle controversy, will compromise their larger goals of ending the capitalistic system, but they decide in favor of the boycott. Many leftist groups undoubtedly joined the boycott for reasons similar to those expressed here. Other groups had completely different reasons for joining.

451. World Health Organization.
"International Code of Marketing of Breastmilk Substitutes." Reprint. New York: Interfaith Center on Corporate Responsibility, 1981.
Distributed by ICCR, this shortened and annotated version of the WHO Code regulating breastmilk substitutes highlights the particular provisons which the critic groups consider important.

E. CHURCH PUBLICATIONS

452. "Allin Sets Framework in Nestle Controversy." *Diocesan Press Service,* #81057. New York: Episcopal Church Center, February 19, 1981.
This article contains observations by Presiding Bishop John M. Allin of The Episcopal Church in early 1981 in which he counsels constructive dialogue between Nestle and its opponents and urges that the dispute be set in the larger context of efforts to improve economic conditions and achieve better public health results in less-developed countries.

453. Anderson, Ann.
"Presbyterians Urge Boycott of Nestle." *Missionscope* No. 6, June 1979. The author reports that the United Presbyterian Church, through its 191st General Assembly, approved a resolution, May 30, 1979, to join in a boycott of the services and products of the Nestle Company.

454. Beck, Roy Howard.
"Infant Formula Study Starts." *United Methodist Reporter* October 31, 1980. This informational report considers the process by which the United Methodist Church studied the issue of whether or not to support the Nestle boycott. The Methodists set up a task force to solicit information from representatives of both sides of the dispute and from outside consultants in the fields involved. Careful consideration was counseled by Dr. Philip Wogaman, Infant Task Force chairman.

455. Borden, Stanley P.
"Responsible Social Witness." *The American Baptist* (Cleveland News Section), September 1981.
The General Board of the *American Baptist* passed a resolution in the fall of 1981 in support of the Nestle boycott. This presentation states that the process by which the resolution of support was considered and adopted was hasty, unbalanced and irresponsible. One could properly contrast this process with the one followed by the United Methodist Church.

456. Burns, Karen.
Letter, Franciscan Sisters of Allegany. NY: St. Elizabeth Mission Society, Inc., January 3, 1979.
Sister Burns, a former missionary to South America and Mission Procurator of the Franciscan Sisters of Allegany, voices support for Nestle's efforts in Third World countries based on her own personal experiences with Nestle products in Bolivia and South America and the favorable reports received from other missionaries working in the field.

457. "Call for World Health Organization Conference on Infant Feeding." Proposed Resolution of Standing Committee for the Office of Research and Analysis, October 16-17, 1978.
This proposed resolution was recommended to the American Lutheran Church for adoption. Instead of joining in the boycott, this resolution called for the Church to endorse the idea of an international conference on infant feeding, in light of Nestle's willingness to participate in such a conference.

458. Early, Tracy.
"Why Boycott Nestle: Testing the Case for the Defense." *Christianity and Crisis* 38:172, June 25, 1979.
Beginning with a modest review of the bibliographic sources on the Nestle controversy, this essay discusses the Nestle print and public relations campaign, calling it a diversion from the real issue. It is a cynical evaluation of Nestle's motives in the controversy. It concludes with a discussion of the INFACT campaign and lists Nestle products to be avoided.

459. Early, Tracy.
"Nothing New with Nestle." *A.D. 1980* United Presbyterian Church 9(5):19, May 1980.
This brief article generally discusses the issues of the boycott. It attempts objectivity by including mild criticisms of anti-Nestle activists, particularly INFACT, but the overall tone is hostile towards Nestle, relying on the typical arguments voiced by Nestle's critics.

460. Ellwood, Gracia Fay.
"Death in a Baby Bottle." *The Reformed Journal* p. 15, June 1978.
This is a lengthy, popular discussion of the developing controversy over formula sales in the Third World, but one which presumes that a boycott is in order. This article was also reprinted in *Presbyterian Survey* 68:19, August 1978.

461. Fisher, Paul A.
"New Formula for Revolution: Babies and the Church." *The Wanderer* 114(45), November 5, 1981.
In reviewing the developing Nestle controversy in churches, the author argues that this is just another issue by activists with a socialist bent. He opposes this development and states that, while firms are not without fault, they provide services for which people ought to be grateful.

462. Howell, Leon.
"A New Maturity for the Infant Formula Debate." *Christianity and Crisis* March 16, 1981.
In discussing the pending WHO meeting in Geneva, this article notes the views of both sides in the dispute. It emphasizes the "leaked" memo written by a Nestle official on the subject of company strategy and its effects. The article supports Nestle's opponents.

463. Lytle, William P., William P. Thompson and G. Daniel Little.
Letter from the United Presbyterian Church in the United States of America, General Assembly Mission Council, September 1979.
Following the decision of the United Presbyterian Church to join in the Nestle boycott in 1979, this letter and other communications were sent out explaining the action and telling the recipient where further information about the controversy could be obtained.

464. Minus, Paul M.
"Infant Formula Issue: Other Perspectives: Boycott of Nestle." *Christian Century* 96:662, June 20, 1979.
In an attempt to foster interest in the religious community, this essay explains the growing controversy among church leaders over the infant formula issue. It does caution against seeing the dispute as a simple "good guys-bad guys" issue, and calls for the involvement of more church people.

465. "Nestle's New Crunch: The Presbyterian Boycott."
*A.D.*p. 40, September 1979.
Many church publications kept close touch with the boycott that they had joined by resolution. This interview is with Mrs. Patricia Young, a member of ICCR, as she responds to questions about the boycott. The answers represent the emphasis of Nestle's opponents against the promotion of the formula. Questions also deal with the effectiveness of such an approach.

466. "Nestle Offers Support of World Health Code."
United Methodist Reporter 9(34), July 31, 1981.
After the announcement that Nestle will support the WHO Code, the United Methodist Church said that it would hold its regular fall meeting at a hotel in Dayton, Ohio owned by a Nestle subsidiary.

467. "Nestle Boycott, Mediation Efforts, and Christian Ethical Teaching."
United Methodist Reporter October 30, 1981.
This editorial points out that the United Methodist Church's Council on Ministries is receiving criticism for its patient inquiry into the

Nestle controversy and its unwillingness to join the Nestle boycott. The church body is playing an important part in obtaining real change without over-simplifying the issues.

468. Richardson, Jean L.
"Countering Infant Formula Promotion." *The Christian Century* p.708, July 19-26, 1978.
The writer of this letter advocates the petitioning of the Food and Drug Administration in the United States to require labeling of formula containers advising that formula is not like breast milk. Furthermore, this writer demands that sampling, even to physicians, be curtailed.

469. Schoonmaker, Mary E.
"Infant Formula: The Hard Sell Works Here, Too." *Christianity and Crisis* 41:213, July 20, 1981.
The article notes that the baby formula controversy, though focused in the Third World, also affects babies in the United States, citing the San Francisco Public Advocate law firm's efforts to restrict formula marketing.

470. United Methodist Communications News.
"Infant Formula." Indianapolis: The News Service of the U.M. Church, no date.
This news release, circulated by the United Methodist Church, announces that the church's Infant Formula Task Force endorses the WHO Code regulating the sale of infant formula. The release discusses the process used by the Task Force to arrive at its decision to support the Code. The release is a useful source of information about the Task Force's approach to the dispute.

F. INFANT FOOD INDUSTRY PUBLICATIONS

471. Abbott/Ross Laboratories.
"Policy on Clinical Samples of Infant Formula in Developing Countries." Chicago: Abbott Laboratories, March 1978.
These guidelines govern the use of samples of Abbott products. Samples are not to be used to induce mothers to abandon breastfeeding and to begin formula feeding unless a health professional has so advised the mother. Samples should not be given to mothers who cannot afford the use of formula. It is up to distributors to properly monitor and control the uses to which samples are put and to report any violations of the sampling guidelines.

472. Abbott/Ross Laboratories.
"Current Concerns Regarding Infant Formula in Developing Countries." Chicago: Abbott Laboratories, 1978.
This manufacturer of infant formula explains its position that although breastfeeding in early infancy is best, the use of properly prepared commercial infant formula can make an important contribution to the health and well-being of infants worldwide. The issues of

discouraging mothers from breastfeeding, formula advertising and Abbott's response to these issues are presented.

473. Abbott/Ross Laboratories.
"The Abbott Laboratories Respond to Third World Issues." Chicago: Abbott Laboratories, June 1979.

This brief statement outlines the position of Abbott Laboratories on a number of questions concerning promotion of infant formula to less-developed countries. Abbott early (1972) issued a Code of Marketing Ethics which required the cessation of all forms of consumer advertising, discouragement of sales where the use of the formula would cause economic hardship, and the promotion of breastfeeding as the first choice in infant feeding. The Ross Laboratories Division of Abbott also established a Third World Task Force to visit problem areas, conduct research and oversee the sale of formula in less-developed countries.

474. Abbott/Ross Laboratories.
"Mothers in Conflict — Children in Need." Columbus: Third World Research Dept., Ross Laboratories Division, July 1979.

This is a flier for a film produced by Abbott Laboratories entitled "Mothers in Conflict — Children in Need." The central theme of the film is that the promotion and availability of commercial formula in less-developed countries cannot be considered to be the major factor in influencing the decision of the Third World mother to bottle or breast-feed.

475. Abbott/Ross Laboratories.
"Breast-Feeding and Audiocassette Order Form" (with attached interoffice memo). Columbus: Ross Laboratories, October 1980.

Posters, each showing mothers breastfeeding their infant clad according to their national group, were made available by Ross Laboratories. Each has captions in various national languages. Attached is a memo showing the ordering of these posters which took place by distributors in various countries from Guam to Chile.

476. Abbott/Ross Laboratories.
"Abbott/Ross Laboratories' Position on the World Health Organization International Code of Marketing of Breast Milk Substitutes." Chicago: Abbott Laboratories, June 1981.

Following the adoption in May 1981 of the WHO Code of Marketing of Breastmilk Substitutes, Abbott/Ross Laboratories issued this provision-by-provision analysis of the WHO Code. Generally, the analysis views the Code as failing to address the fundamental scientific problems of infant feeding in the less-developed world. The Code is overly restrictive and gives the false impression that the infant formula industry created the problems of infant disease and malnutrition and failed to take corrective action when called upon to do so.

477. Abbott/Ross Laboratories.
"The Weakness of the Scientific Premises Underlying the W.H.O. Code for Marketing of Breastmilk Substitutes." Chicago: Abbott Laboratories, March 1981, updated July 1981.

This updated version of an earlier report is virtually the same as that earlier report of March 1981. In it the writers dispute the "erroneous premises" on which the WHO Code was based.

478. Abbott Laboratories, American Home Products Corporation and Bristol-Myers Company.
"Joint Position by Abbott Laboratories, American Home Products Corporation, and Bristol-Myers Company Concerning the World Health Organization's Proposed International Marketing Code for Breastmilk Substitutes." Columbus, Ohio: Ross Laboratories, March 1981.

Three companies which produce formula join in this statement opposing United States adoption of the WHO Code of Marketing of Breastmilk Substitutes. The companies state these reasons, among others, for joining in opposition to the Code: There is no evidence that marketing formula has led to a decline in breastfeeding. The "recommendation" form of the Code can be converted into a more binding document. The Code severely and in an unwarranted way restricts legitimate commercial activities contrary to the principles and ideals of the United States.

479. Abbott Laboratories, American Home Products Corporation and Bristol-Myers Company.
"The Weakness of the Scientific Premises Underlying the W.H.O. Code for Marketing of Breastmilk Substitutes." Columbus, Ohio: Ross Laboratories, March 1981.

The writers describe three erroneous premises upon which the "WHO Code of Marketing of Breastmilk Substitutes" was based. They are: that breastfeeding is declining; that marketing practices of infant formula companies have affected mothers' choices for breast versus formula feeding; and that the use of infant formula is necessarily harmful. The authors then refer to scientific studies which support their contention that the WHO Code was passed on the basis of erroneous assumptions. The WHO Code should not supported says this report.

480. Abbott Laboratories, American Home Products Corporation and Bristol-Myers Company.
"World Health Organization Development of An International Code for the Marketing of Infant Formulas: Background and Perspective." Columbus, Ohio: Ross Laboratories, March 1981.

According to this paper, breast milk from a well-nourished mother can meet the nutritional needs of infants for from four to six months, while a poorly nourished mother may have adequate milk for the infant only up until two or three months. Infant formula used as a supplement is superior to many alternatives to breast milk which have been used. The writers cite the Protein Advisory Group's (United Nations) Statement #23 as taking a sensible position on infant feeding. The WHO drafts of its marketing Code are reviewed. The first draft was full of unwarranted and absolute prohibitions on commercial activities. Full intergovernmental negotiations were asked for by the United States if a Code was to be developed. WHO, however, did not follow that procedure. The following reasons for opposition to the WHO Code are set out: there is no substantial evidence which shows that the final draft of the Code would improve infant nutrition and health, and there is no substantial evidence that the sale of infant formula has contributed to the decline of breastfeeding.

481. American Home Products Corporation.
"Notice of Annual Meeting of Stockholders." New York: American Home Products Corporation, March 20, 1978.
This notice of the annual stockholders meeting and proxy statement carries a stockholders resolution against the promotional practices of American Home Products in its sale of infant formula to less-developed countries. The management of the company indicates that it recommends a vote against the resolution and outlines its reasons for opposition.

482. American Home Products Corporation.
"Notice of Annual Meeting of Stockholders." New York: American Home Products Corporation, March 16, 1979.
In 1978 a resolution against American Home Products' promotion of infant formula in less-developed countries had been proposed.This proposed resolution is another on the same subject. The reasons for the resolution are provided as well as the company's response which cites company testimony and carries a typical label for "SMA," infant formula distributed by the company.

483. American Home Products Corporation.
"Infant Formula in Developing Countries." New York: American Home Products Corporation, 1981.
This brief statement by American Home Products states that breast milk is best; however, if breast milk is not in sufficient supply, a formula supplement should be used. The company advises against a "watchdog committee" proposed by the Interfaith Center on Corporate Responsibility. The publication includes sample illustrations of non-verbal instructions for preparing formula, which are part of infant formula labels.

484. Barter, I.S.
"The Infant Food Industry." *Lancet* 2(8086):421, August 19, 1978.
Mr. Barter, President of ICIFI, states that ICIFI is ready to participate in a standing conference on infant feeding products. Legitimate and practical solutions to the several problems which have been raised can be achieved by such exchange.

485. Bristol-Myers Company.
"Statements of the Sisters of the Precious Blood and Bristol-Myers Company on Infant Formula Marketing Practices Overseas." New York: Mead Johnson and Company, c. 1978.
This publication contains alternating statements by the Sisters of the Precious Blood and Bristol-Myers Company. The Sisters had pursued a stockholder's resolution against the promotion of infant formula by Bristol-Myers in less-developed countries. After various legal maneuvers, both parties agreed to a settlement including the issuance of this statement in which the Sisters and Bristol-Myers explain their respective points of view. The Sisters' position was the marketing of infant formula in less-developed countries could result in malnutrition and disease. The company, while recognizing the need for close scrutiny of sales, nevertheless believes that the precautions taken by the company and the informed choice of mothers in less-developed coun-

tries have sufficiently guaranteed that formula will be a healthful addition to the Third World.

486. Bristol-Myers Company.
"Stockholder Proposals — Infant Formulas (I) & (II)." Annual Report of the Board of Directors and Proxy Solicitation, Bristol-Myers Company, April 1980.
Bristol-Myers had two different resolutions presented to it, both dealing with some aspect of the infant formula controversy. Although the company had stopped consumer advertising and "milk nurses," an additional resolution dealt with sampling of formula and promotion to health personnel. A second resolution would have required Bristol-Myers to issue a report on sales and promotion practices in the United States and Canada. Bristol-Myers argues that the availability of formula does not discourage breastfeeding.

487. Bristol-Myers Company.
"No Link Between Infant Formula Marketing Practices and Bottle Feeding in Third World, AID Report Says." *Second Quarter Report,* 1981.
In its second quarterly report to stockholders, Bristol-Myers presents two pages of arguments against the WHO Code. It offers to its shareholders copies of an AID report and the WHO's Collaborative Study on Breastfeeding. According to this report the WHO Code does not address and will not solve the problems of infants in the Third World.

488. Bristol-Myers Company.
"Policies and Practices: Production, Labeling and Marketing of Infant Formula Products in Countries Outside the U.S.A. (including its possessions) and Canada." Bristol-Myers Company, International Division, c. 1981.
This internal set of instructions was given to distributors of infant formula outside the United States and Canada. The practices and policies required are (1) product labeling which encourages breastfeeding first and proper instructions, (2) marketing only through health care workers, and to those who can afford it, (3) the prohibition of mass-marketing and (4) close contact with local health and governmental officials.

489. Ciocca, Henry G.
"The Infant Formula Controversy." *Journal of Contemporary Business* 7:37, 1979.
This article argues that the problems of infant nutrition are more complex than opposition groups have made the issues. The piece explains Nestle's part in industry-wide initiatives to monitor formula promotion practices, the scientific evidence which favors the cautious promotion of formula through health professionals, the general decline in mortality in less-developed countries despite increasing formula usage, and the absolute dangers of unsupplemented breastfeeding.

490. Ciocca, Henry G.
"The Nestle Boycott as a Corporate Learning Experience." The Nestle Company, Inc. First presented to the Institute of Food Technology, Northeast Section, March 18, 1980.
This pamphlet, published by Nestle, outlines its view of the controversy, including actions by its opponents and by its own staff as the

events unfolded.The author was directly involved in making policy decisions about the dispute in its earlier stages.

491. Cox, David O.
"A Perspective on Infant Formula in Developing Countries." Paper presented at MIT-Harvard International Nutrition Planning Seminar, May 12, 1980.
Cox points to population growth, evidence that breastfeeding is still the overwhelming choice of rural and urban women in less-developed countries, and various reasons which Third World women give for shifting to artificial feeding to show that the promotional efforts of infant formula companies have not been primarily responsible for what changes have occurred in infant feeding practices. In addition, Cox explains the steps Ross Laboratories has taken to control advertising and promotion.

492. Cox, David O.
"The Infant Formula Controversy: Galileo Revisited." Lecture presented at the School of Organization and Management, Yale University, March 26, 1981.
The writer reviews the many positions taken by researchers on infant feeding questions. He emphasizes that mixed feeding seems to be the most common mode of feeding today in the less-developed world. He states that studies show that the decisions about early infant feeding are complex and that there is difficulty in extracting one variable which is significant to such decisions. The writer also describes the WHO Code process as overly political.

493. Cox, David O.
"The Infant Formula Issue: A Case Study." In: Epstein, Edwin M. and Lee E. Preston, eds., Business Environment/Public Policy: The Field and Its Future. (Proceeding of the AACSB Summer Conference). St. Louis, Missouri: American Assembly of Collegiate Schools of Business, 1981.
The writer explains the need for infant formula in the less-developed world by explaining the under-nourishment, low birth weight, and poor milk production of many Third World mothers. He reviews the charges made against the formula manufacturers and the affirmative steps taken by Ross Laboratories to promote breastfeeding as a part of infant care.

494. International Council of Infant Food Industries.
Press Communique, Japan, 1978.
This press communique provides information about the meeting of ICIFI in Tokyo in 1978. Four new member firms were accepted into the organization. Progress was reported on implementation of U.N. PAG Statement #23.

495. "International Council of Infant Food Industries: Its Aims and Progress." Lancet 8076:1250, June 10, 1978.
The editors of The Lancet give space to ICIFI to make a statement about the efforts they are making at self-regulation. Its statement gives a brief history of the trade association and then explains its intention to study infant feeding and act on the basis of its findings. This summary is important in understanding the controversy because it shows early industry views and concerns.

496. International Council of Infant Food Industries.
"Supplementary Background Paper and Recommendations." P.O.B. 328, CH-8035 and FHE/ICF/REP/1-5/Rev. 3, Zurich, Switzerland: Submitted to WHO/UNICEF "Meeting on Infant and Young Child Feeding." Geneva, October 9-12, 1979.

In the fall of 1979 the International Council of Infant Food Industries, of which Nestle was a member, published a long and well-documented paper to be distributed to those participating in the "Meeting on Infant and Young Child Feeding" to be conducted in October of 1979, jointly by the World Health Organization and UNICEF. The infant food industry took the position that infant formula was appropriate as both a supplement and as a substitute in certain circumstances and that efforts to restrict general access to Third World peoples to formula was unwarranted. The paper also challenges the view that the marketing of infant formula has had an adverse effect on infant mortality trends in the less-developed world. Certain studies are openly questioned due to imperfect design or the collection of ambiguous data.

497. International Council of Infant Food Industries.
"Is the Industry Observing the Recommendations?: The Facts." The WHO/UNICEF Meeting on Infant and Young Child Feeding, August 1980.

ICIFI published this brochure to counter the charges made by critic groups that Nestle and other companies were in repeated violation of the Recommendations made by WHO/UNICEF in 1979. Of 117 cases affecting ICIFI companies, say the writers, only 15 appeared to be justified. On those counts corrective action was taken at once. The other cases were exaggerated, completely misleading, or too vague to permit investigation, according to the authors of this publication. (Later the Infant Formula Nestle Audit Commission is formed to deal with this problem).

498. "An Interview with Arthur Furer, President of Nestle, S.A." *Tages Anzeiger* October 19, 1979

In this interview, Arthur Furer of Nestle speaks about the results of the 1979 WHO/UNICEF Conference. The responses are direct and very interesting because they have been often quoted out of context in the popular campaign. For example, Furer says in an often quoted statement that Nestle does not feel restricted by the WHO recommendations. However, he points out that the reason for this is that the changes which Nestle has gradually introduced correspond to the recommendations. Mr. Furer's answers stress the contributions which Nestle has made to the decline of infant mortality in developing countries.

499. Jackson, Thad M.
"Nestle Discusses the Recommended WHO Infant Formula Code." Testimony given before Subcommittees of the Foreign Affairs Committee, U.S. House of Representatives, June 16, 1981.

Nestle nutrition expert Dr. Thad Jackson gave the substance of this testimony before a subcommittee in the U.S. House of Representatives. The testimony is a brief review of the Nestle position that the company will abide by the decisions of individual governments which have national codes and by new codes, including WHO's Code, if such codes should be adopted by individual countries. In this statement Nestle endorses the aim of the WHO Code without agreeing fully with each provision.

500. Nestle.
"Nestle Infant Food Policy." Switzerland: Infant and Dietetic Products Dept., Nestle Products Technical Assistance Co., Ltd., Switzerland, February 1978.
This is a four-page summary of what might be called the Nestle philosophy of infant feeding. According to the document, breastfeeding is to be encouraged during the first few months of infancy. Other elements are discussed such as health services, instruction and educational material.

501. Nestle.
"The Infant Formula Controversy: A Nestle View." White Plains, NY: The Nestle Company, Inc., November 1978.
This is one of many items of information and argument written and distributed by the Nestle Co., Inc., sometimes referred to as "U.S. Nestle". The arguments presented in this publication are that infant mortality is not generally increasing in less-developed countries, that certain data on morbidity are lacking, that in some areas breastfeeding may be declining (though the information to draw such conclusions is incomplete), and that the factors which have produced a decline in breastfeeding in some areas have been multifarious. The publication also argues that a clear distinction should be made between what some call "bottle feeding", which could be the bottle feeding of native weaning foods as well as the bottle feeding of commercial formula. The piece also proposes certain research questions that need answering before solid conclusions can be drawn about formula feeding and supplementary feeding.

502. Nestle.
"Nestle Booklet on Infant Nutrition." Vevey, Switzerland: Nestle S.A., Nestle Publications, New Series No. 1, 1978.
This booklet, published by Nestle, summarizes the firm's views of the problem of formula feeding and breastfeeding. The booklet makes use of extensive pictorial and graphic material.

503. Nestle.
A Decade of Practical Work by the Nestle Foundation in the Ivory Coast, 1969-1979. Vevey, Switzerland: Nestle Foundation, March 31, 1979.
This is a Nestle Foundation report on its efforts in the Ivory Coast to improve the dietary quality of that nation's food. It must be considered as an example of motives which are broader and longer-ranging than "quick profits".

504. Nestle.
"Nestle and Infant Formula: Facts and Fallacies." Washington, D.C.: Nestle Coordination Center for Nutrition, Inc., April 1979.
This publication uses a "point/counter-point" style to discuss controversial subjects such as infant mortality, promotional activities, milk nurses and free samples to physicians.

505. Nestle.
"Infant Nutrition in Developing Countries: A Nestle View." White Plains, NY: Nestle Company, Inc., May 1979.
This publication, written and circulated by the Nestle Company, Inc. (U.S. Nestle), is a revision of an earlier publication entitled "The Infant Formula Controversy: A Nestle View". The arguments are basically the same as those in the earlier version, but here they are more fully developed and, for the researcher, more extensively footnoted and documented. Nestle argues that infant mortality and morbidity have not increased in less-developed countries and that breastfeeding, where it has declined, has been caused by factors that have little to do with Nestle. The paper voices continued concern over certain distortions that Nestle believes have been introduced into the debate by its opponents.

506. Nestle.
"How Nestle Has Followed the WHO/UNICEF October 1979 Recommendations." Vevey, Switzerland: Nestle S.A., April 1981.
This summary by Nestle on what it has done in specific cases or complaints since 1979 is in response to criticisms leveled against it by its opponents.

507. Nestle.
Aide Memoire I. Washington, D.C.: Nestle Coordination Center for Nutrition, September 25, 1981.
This memo to the United Methodist Church Infant Formula Task Force contains Nestle's position in favor of having individual countries adopt or adapt the WHO Code. It also contains the proposal that the Methodist Task Force serve as a conduit for channeling alleged violations of the WHO Code to Nestle.

508. Pagan, Rafael D.
"Nestle — A Corporation Maligned." Washington, D.C.: Nestle Coordination Center for Nutrition, Inc., November 11, 1981.
In this speech Pagan sets the Nestle boycott in the context of a general anti-business mentality which opposes business enterprises wherever the opportunity presents itself. He views most American church people as moderates who will listen to Nestle's case that international corporations, although not perfect, are the best hope for development and wealth creation in the less-developed world. Finally, Pagan urges businessmen to listen to their critics, to answer them forthrightly, and not to apologize for what they are doing when they are convinced that they are right.

509. Sarett, Herbert P.
"Indications for Use of Infant Formula." New York: Bristol-Myers, Mead Johnson Nutritional Division, October 1979.
This statement outlines maternal and infant conditions where breastfeeding is not recommended and, thus, infant formula is appropriate. These include the mother's death or illness, the production of insufficient milk, infant illness where weight-loss has occurred, and cases where the infant has a low birth weight.

510. Wyeth International, Ltd.
"Statement of Wyeth International Limited." Presented at the WHO/UNICEF Meeting on Infant and Young Child Feeding. Geneva, October 9-12, 1979.
This paper provides, among other things, a listing of instances where infants at high risk need additional nutrients. The general position of Wyeth is that breastfeeding should be the first choice for the infant, however, when breast milk is unavailable or insufficient, infant formula should be used with appropriate guidance. Instances where infant formula is needed are: infant's mother has died or has an active infection like tuberculosis or malaria; infant is fed by a child minder; infant's mother does not produce adequate milk, and others.

511. Wyeth Laboratories.
"Wyeth Hospital Infant Feeding System." New York: American Home Products Corporation, Wyeth Laboratories, October 1981.
This publication from Wyeth presents the history of the development of Wyeth feeding products for infants, reviews each of the products, its chemical make-up and nutritional benefits, and then lists specialized products for infants who cannot tolerate a high renal load or are suffering, for example, from leucine-sensitive hypoglycemia.

IV. THE PHASE OF THE WHO CODE AND THE INDUSTRY RESPONSE: 1982-1983

A. GENERAL ARTICLES AND STUDIES

512. Adelman, Carol.
"Infant Formula, Science and Politics." *Policy Review #23*. Washington, D.C.: The Heritage Foundation, Winter 1983.
This article considers the views formed by pediatric organizations and physicians, in the latter portion of the controversy, on the available scientific evidence. The article is highly readable, despite its references to scholarly sources.

513. Adelman, Kenneth.
"Biting the Hand that Cures Them." *Regulation*. (American Enterprise Institute Journal on Government and Society) July/August 1982.
The campaign against infant formula companies is part of a larger effort to regulate the sale of other products to Third World countries, especially drug sales, says Adelman. He also discusses drugs which, though banned in the United States, are sold elsewhere, including the less-developed world.

514. Andersson, Mari.
"To Advocate or Not to Advocate Is the Question." *Press Woman* May 1983.
This piece offers quotations from scientific sources which counter the charges made against Nestle. The author, a journalist and editor of medical and church publications, petitioned the United Methodist Church not to support the boycott.

515. Ball, Robert.
"The Formula Crisis Cools." *Fortune* 106:106, December 27, 1982.
The author reports on the progress of the controversy, stating that efforts against Nestle seem to be winding down. The writer gives a brief review of the apparent attitudes and strategies of Nestle in the dispute.

516. Barovick, Richard L.
"Activism on a Global Scale." *Public Relations Journal* p. 29, June 1982.
Barovick's article discusses groups and networks which have supported the Nestle boycott. He speaks of publications such as the *Multinational Monitor,* and groups such as Institute for Policy Studies, Infant Formula Action Coalition, Interfaith Center on Corporate Responsibility, and International Baby Food Action Network. The author examines steps which Nestle has taken — the opening of the Nestle Coordination Center for Nutrition, the issuing of compliance instructions for observance of the WHO Code, and the establishment of an Audit Commission to review allegations that Nestle violated WHO or national marketing codes.

517. Beauchamp, Tom L.
Case Studies in Business, Society, and Ethics. Englewood Cliffs, NJ: Prentice-Hall, Inc., 1983.
The author includes a case study of the Nestle formula feeding controversy. Newly available information about the Nestle Audit Commission and other recent developments are not included, but some scientific evidence is mentioned.

518. Bickerstaffe, George.
"New Leadership Rouses Sleeping Giant Nestle." *International Marketing: Europe* February 1983.
In November 1981, Helmut Maucher became the managing director of Nestle. This article concerns the change he brought to top management. Of the formula feeding controversy, he states that elements which made up the dispute — baby, breast, multinational, and Third World — coalesced to make the issues very enduring and difficult. The article repeatedly refers to Maucher's "provocative management" outlook.

519. Chetley, Andy.
"There's No Substitute for Mothers' Milk." *World Health* p. 12, February/March 1983.
The author gives the reader information about formula feeding in parts of Bangladesh. The account concerns two infants, one who was formula fed and the other who was breastfed. There are quotations from a local doctor who headed the community health clinic stating that he is opposed to bottle feeding even among urban mothers. The clinics and health workers encourage breastfeeding.

520. David, Peter.
"Barbados — Promotion Fails." *Ideas Forum* No. 15, 1983-84.
Beginning in 1969, health professionals in Barbados ran an intensive educational campaign promoting breastfeeding. There was evidence

that mothers generally knew the advantages of breastfeeding after the completion of the education program. The number of mothers breastfeeding, however, declined. The author explains that a substantial portion of the mothers did not have a live-in husband or relative upon whom to rely for emotional support and assistance around the house. Mothers were anxious, therefore, to get the baby accustomed to bottle feeding in order to handle household tasks and to work more efficiently.

521. Donaldson, Thomas.
Corporations and Morality. Englewood Cliffs, NJ: Prentice-Hall, Inc., 1982.
The Nestle controversy is given as an example of a business bearing an indirect moral obligation. Because they know of the improper preparation or use of a product which they are selling, they must take precautions to keep that from happening, the author says. The industry's attempts to deal with these problems are not mentioned.

522. Fikentscher, Wolfgang.
"United Nations Codes of Conduct: New Paths in International Law." 30 *Americal Journal of Comparative Law* 577, Fall 1982.
The author discusses international regulatory codes, including the Infant Formula Code adopted by WHO in May 1981. His major point is that sanctions under the Code are weak, but that if a nation were to adopt the Code, the Code provisions could be used as a basis for bringing a tort suit against a formula manufacturing company.

523. Higgins, Kevin.
"Infant Formula Protest Teaches Nestle a Tactical Lesson." *Marketing News* 17(12):1, June 10, 1983.
In a discussion of Nestle's changing tactics in the formula controversy, this article reports the success of Nestle's aggressive head-on campaign against its critics.

524. Maletnlema, T.N.
"How Will You Feed Your Baby in the 80s?" Tanzania Food and Nutrition Centre, *TFNC Report* #445.
The author of this lengthy report is opposed to Nestle (or any other infant formula corporation) operating in Tanzania. He argues that breastfeeding and traditional Tanzanian weaning foods are sufficient to raise healthy babies without the importation of Western powdered formulas.

525. Miller, Fred D., Jr.
Out of the Mouths of Babes: The Infant Formula Controversy. Bowling Green, Ohio: The Social Philosophy and Policy Center, Bowling Green State University, 1983.
This booklet analyzes the controversy through review of studies of infant feeding practices worldwide. The author identifies the failings that often exist in these studies because of faulty collection of data, improper inference, and extreme localism of sample. The book explores the ethical assumptions of those who prefer to have infant feeding choices overseen by governmental and international agencies. The writer also disputes the view that Western advertising has foisted unneeded and unwanted products on Third World peoples.

526. Sparks, John A.
The Nestle Controversy — Another Look. Grove City, PA: Public Policy Education Fund, Inc., 1982.
This pamphlet, which traces the Nestle controversy from its beginnings in the early 1970s through 1982, exposes the reader to materials and articles on the questions involved and includes endnotes for further reading. The pamphlet summarizes the arguments of health experts on weaning foods and breastfeeding.

Note: The substance of this pamphlet is reprinted in *Food Policy* 5(3):220, August 1980, a quarterly published by IPC Science and Technology Press, Ltd. A rejoinder by Andy Chetley of London's War on Want follows this reprint.

527. United States House Committee on Foreign Affairs.
"Implementation of the WHO Code on Infant Formula Marketing Practices: Hearings, June 16 and 17, 1981, before the Subcommittees on International Economic Policy and Trade and on Human Rights and International Organizations", 1982 iv+ 175 pp.
The U.S. position on the International Code of Marketing of Breast Milk Substitutes, adopted by WHO, May 1981, was the subject of this House Subcommittee hearing. Representatives of the industry, scientists, and representatives of the Department of State and the Department of Health and Human Services testified, as well as other interested parties.

528. Valasquez, Manuel G.
"Marketing Infant Formula." In: Business and Ethics. Englewood Cliffs, NJ: Prentice-Hall, Inc., 1982.
In this textbook, a presentation is made of the formula feeding controversy. The author obviously intended to give only an introduction to the dispute. Varying views are contrasted, but later developments, such as the Nestle Audit Commission, are not included.

B. SCIENTIFIC ARTICLES AND STUDIES

529. Ashworth, A., S. R. Allen and G. A. Fookes.
"Infant and Young Child Feeding — A Selected Annotated Bibliography."
Early Human Development (Supplement) Vol. 6, April 1982.
This selected annotated bibliography covers a ten-year period, 1972-1982, but gives greater attention to scientific materials from 1977 on. The authors provide summaries of articles, studies, or papers, often with tabulated findings. The bibliography is broken into eleven major classifications with subdivisions related to aspects of early infant nutrition. Major categories include maternal supplementation, breastfeeding, breast milk, contamination, weaning, morbidity and mortality. Under breastfeeding, the annotators include subdivisions on adequacy of breast milk, attitudes toward breastfeeding, as well as sub-sections on economic aspects of breastfeeding.

530. Bellanti, Joseph A., ed.
Acute Diarrhea: Its Nutritional Consequences in Children. Nestle Nutrition Workshop Series, Vol. 2. New York: Raven Press, 1983.
This is a collection of papers presented at a conference on "Acute

Diarrhea: Its Nutritional Consequences in Children," held in May 1982. The chapters first discuss the public health and epidemiological problems of diarrhea in children. Then new viral, bacterial and parasitic agents are discussed. The nutritional consequences of diarrhea and the relationship between types of feeding and diarrhea are presented. Finally, means of treating diarrhea, including oral rehydration and anti-diarrheal vaccines, are offered and evaluated.

531. Dobbing, John.
"Breast Is Best — Isn't It?" Paper read to a Symposium on Health Hazards of Milk at the University of Manchester, September 13-14, 1983.
Dobbing begins his analysis of the case for breastfeeding by stating that though breastfeeding is best, it is not best because of exaggerated claims based on limited evidence. All studies comparing breastfed infants with artificially fed infants contain a fundamental fallacy, he says. The two populations select themselves rather than being selected at random. Commercially prepared formula, moreover, is sometimes compared with cow's milk when in reality most formulas are adapted so that they come very close to human milk's composition. The author says that malnourished mothers who engage in manual labor cannot lactate adequately for six months. He also points out that supplementation of the mothers' diets while they are lactating does not seem to improve lactation. The writer discusses immunology and breastfeeding, infant-mother bonding and other defenses for breastfeeding.

532. Greiner, Ted and Michael D. Latham.
"The Influence of Infant Food Advertising on Infant Feeding Practices in St. Vincent." *International Journal of Health Services* 12(1):53, 1982.
After interviewing the mothers of about 200 children in the eastern Caribbean, the authors conclude that mothers who had been influenced by infant food advertising were more likely to bottle feed their infants earlier than other mothers. The authors warn about the constraints and limits of the study. The article demonstrates how many technical problems must be dealt with by those who try to measure the choices that mothers make on the question of breast versus formula feeding.

533. Helsing, Elizabeth and F. Savage King.
Breast-Feeding in Practice: A Manual for Health Workers. New York: Oxford University Press, 1982.
The authors set out to answer the many questions attendant to breastfeeding, once answered by mothers and grandmothers, but which now are often perplexing because of the prevalence of formula feeding. The book is largely non-political.

534. Hofvander, Y., et al.
"The Amount of Milk Consumed by 1-3 Months Old Breast-or-Bottle-Fed Infants." *Acta Paediatrica Scandinavica* 71:953, 1982.
The authors conclude that with babies who are bottle feeding, just as with those who are breastfeeding, there is a built-in biological mechanism which enables the infant to demand more or less nourishment to meet his bodily needs. The article says that measurement of milk intake is still best estimated by weighing the infant before and after feeding.

535. Manderson, Lenore.
"Bottle Feeding and Ideology in Colonial Malaya: The Production of Change."
International Journal of Health Services 12(4):597, 1982.
This article reviews the marketing of condensed milk and infant
formula in Malaya. The author concludes that artificial feeds were
sold and advertised from the late 19th century on, first to English-
speaking persons and then to native Malaysians. At the same time,
other social and cultural factors discouraged breastfeeding. Formula
feeding was well-established before the intensive promotion of infant
formula by multinational corporations following independence.

536. Paine, Randolph and R. J. Coble.
"Breast-Feeding and Infant Health in a Rural U.S. Community." *American
Journal of Diseases in Childhood* 136(1):36, January 1982.
During the first month of life, a significant difference was found in the
number of office visits for illness between breastfed infants and infants
who were bottle fed from birth. At six months of life, similar findings
were reported. Demographic corrections were made in the two groups.
The conclusion is that breastfeeding offers a protective advantage
against illness.

537. Popesco, Cathy Becker.
"Breast or Bottle?" Summit, NJ: American Council on Science and Health,
July 1983.
This pamphlet recommends that mothers breastfeed their infants if
possible. When breast milk is insufficient or must be discontinued,
commercial infant formula can serve as an effective supplement or an
effective alternative to breast milk. The pamphlet also explains that
many of the arguments against infant formula use in underdeveloped
countries do not apply to technologically advanced countries.

538. Popkin, B. M.
"Breast-Feeding Patterns in Low-Income Countries." *Science* 218:1088,
December 10, 1982.
Using data from the World Fertility Survey, the writer concludes that,
on the whole, most children in low-income countries are breastfed for
at least a few months. Limited evidence on trends seems to show that
there has been some decline in the duration of breastfeeding; however,
in most Asian and African countries, breastfeeding is almost universal
during the first six months of the child's life.

C. NEWS ARTICLES

539. Adelman, Carol.
"Saving Babies With a Signature." *Wall Street Journal* July 28, 1982.
Adelman's central point in this editorial is that the adoption of the
World Health Organization's International Code of Marketing of
Breastmilk Substitutes has done little to help malnutrition and health
problems of Third World infants.

540. Andersson, Mari.
"Formula Charges Rebutted." *Journal Herald* (Dayton, OH) March 15, 1982.
This editorial evaluates charges against Nestle and counters with

reference to nutritionists and scientists displeased with the emotional slogans characterizing some of the campaign against Nestle. In keeping with newspaper format, citations in the piece are incomplete.

541. Anzalone, Charles.
"Infant Formula Makers Defend Product Here." *Buffalo Evening News,* June 23, 1982.
The marketing of infant formula is not the cause of declining breastfeeding where such a decline has occurred, says a representative of Bristol-Myers. In addition, this representative cites studies that breastfeeding has not generally declined.

542. Ball, Robert.
"A Shopkeeper Shakes Up Nestle." *Fortune* p. 103, December 27, 1982.
In reporting on Nestle, reference is made to its size, the multinational character of the firm, a drop in its sales, and changes in its management. It discusses the effects of the infant formula controversy on the firm.

543. "The Bottle-or-Breast Debate."
Pittsburgh Post-Gazette May 25, 1982.
This editorial refers to the newly created Audit Commission, or "Muskie Commission," and asks whether it should consider possible loss of life because of the absence of infant formula as well as Nestle's alleged violations of the WHO Code.

544. Carhart, Tom.
"The Nestle Crunch — An Apocryphal Tale." *Washington Times* January 24, 1983.
This review of the controversy, from 1974 to the end of 1983, noted charges by the opponents of Nestle and Nestle's response, including changes in management. The WHO Code will not solve the basic cultural problems that affect formula use, the author concludes.

545. "Challenge From Nestle."
Christian Century p. 328, March 24, 1982.
This item explains a minor picket line confrontation in Baltimore at the site of a Nestle-owned restaurant.

546. Connell, Christopher.
"Nestle Adopts Formula Code." *The Philadelphia Inquirer* 7-A, March 17, 1982.
Nestle's adoption of the WHO Code is the subject here. The publication includes a few remarks about the history of the dispute.

547. "Council Votes to End Nestle Boycott."
American Teacher 67:6, March 1983.
This is a report of the American Federation of Teachers' executive council vote to end the Nestle boycott.

548. deCourcy Hinds, Michael.
"Nestle Revises Policy on Infant Formula." *New York Times* p. C10, March 17, 1982.
This article notes the April 16, 1982 Nestle news release on formula guidelines revision.

549. "The Facts Favor Nestle."
Times-News (Kingsport, TN), October 19, 1982.
After six years of efforts to get Nestle to change its policies (which the author feels have been successful), the activists who fostered the boycott still are maintaining their criticism.

550. Harrigan, Anthony.
"Leftists Stir Attack on Nestle Plan." *Hammond Star* (Los Angeles), February 12, 1982.
This syndicated column recounts the continued complaints against Nestle after its acceptance of the WHO Code.

551. Jenks, Susan.
"Nestle Found Cooperative in Infant Formula Probe." *Washington Times* October 15, 1982.
This is a report of the findings of the Nestle Audit Commission that Nestle has cooperated fully with the Commission in an effort to comply with the WHO Code.

552. Khindaria, Brij.
"WHO Pushes Ban on Promotion of Milk Substitutes." *Financial Times* May 17, 1982.
This article refers to WHO action in which members voted to encourage governments to adopt and implement the WHO Code governing the sale of breast milk substitutes. The Code was adopted a year before this meeting. According to the report, the U.S. voted in favor of such encouragement.

553. Lefever, Ernest W.
"Politics and Baby Formula in the Third World." *Wall Street Journal* p. 26, January 14, 1981.
This editorialist takes the position that formula has made and should continue to make an important contribution to the health and well-being of infants in less-developed countries. If there is to be regulation, it should originate with individual governments, not within the bureaucracies of the U.N. and its agencies. The controversy has been influenced too much by activist groups opposed in principle to multinationals, he says.

554. Madeley, J.
"WHO Wins Battle Over Baby Milk." *Africa* 119:92, July 1981.
This article reports the adoption of the WHO Code in May 1981 as a victory for the WHO in the face of opposition from big business and the U.S. government. The writer praises the work of voluntary groups which he says alerted governments to the danger of formula feeding.

555. Marshall, E.
"Nestle Letter Stops NIH Talk." *Science* 219:469, February 4, 1983.
This story concerns the cancellation of a portion of a National Institute of Health program on the formula feeding controversy. Nestle objected to the inclusion of two speakers known to be opponents of Nestle and refused to send a representative. The incident is interpreted by some as an example of Nestle pressure and by others as proper objection to one-sided programs.

556. McCall, R. B.

"Breast vs. Bottle." *Parents* 57:74, March 1982.

McCall explains the advantages of breastfeeding. In passing he refers to the use of artificial formula in less-developed countries. The piece demonstrates the support from breastfeeding proponents for restrictions upon the marketing of infant formula.

557. Miller, Fred D., Jr.

"Out of the Mouths of Babes." *Barron's* 63(39), September 26, 1983.

The writer reviews the charges of activist groups opposing the marketing of infant formula by multinational firms in the less-developed world and concludes that the scientific evidence for such a stance is weak. He states that, given the responses of the infant formula companies to the WHO Code, the continuing opposition of the activists is based more on ideology than upon hard facts.

558. "More on Nestle."

Christian Century 99:1128, November 10, 1982.

This item comments on the quarterly report of the Muskie Commission.

559. "Muskie to Monitor Nestle on Baby Food."

The New York Times May 5, 1982.

This article relates the creation of the Nestle Audit Commission and its chairing by Edmund Muskie. It also explains the financing of the Commission.

560. "Nestle Agrees to Curtail Advertising of Formula."

The Los Angeles Times March 17, 1982.

This pre-Audit Commission news story announces Nestle's intent to implement the WHO Code. The story reports that boycott supporters are still skeptical about what Nestle will really do.

561. "Nestle Names Panel to Study Infant Formula Controversy."

San Francisco Chronicle May 4, 1982.

This article concerns the announcement of the Nestle Infant Audit Commission. Former Secretary of State Muskie will head it.

562. "Nestle Supports 'Breast is Best' Plan."

Rand Daily Mail March 18, 1982.

This story reports that Nestle will follow specific self-imposed guidelines to comply with the WHO Code on infant formula marketing.

563. "Nestle Takes Healthy Step with New Marketing Formula."

Regina Leader Post March 23, 1982.

This editorial states that Nestle has finally come down on the side of "corporate responsibility" after intense public pressure. The U.S. vote against the WHO Code is cited and, of course, Nestle's statement that it will voluntarily comply with that Code.

564. "Nestle Will Follow Infant Formula Code."

The Chicago Tribune March 17, 1982.

Nestle is reported to be ready to voluntarily implement the WHO Code. The article briefly traces recent developments in the controversy.

565. "Nestle Will Obey Code on Formula."
The Sun (Baltimore) Front page, March 17, 1982.
Nestle is reported as announcing that it will observe the WHO Code.
Dr. Rafael Pagan of Nestle called the changes a quantum jump on the
issue.

566. "Nestle's Offer To Help."
The Arizona Daily Star March 20, 1982.
Nestle is commended in this editorial for its efforts to comply with the
WHO Code.

567. Pagan, Rafael D.
"Nestle and Infant Formula." *Chicago Times* "Perspective" January 11, 1982.
Pagan, the Nestle Coordination Center President, explains that since
1978 Nestle has not marketed infant formula directly to consumers in
less-developed countries. Furthermore, the WHO Code provides for a
grievance system for reporting violations of the Code. Pagan calls for
an end to reckless charges and overstatement.

568. "Revisiting the Formula Fight."
The Washington Post, November 5, 1982.
This editorial says that the data linking formula marketing with
infant mortality is sketchy at best. Common sense, says the editorial,
tells one that the relatively high cost of formula should prevent its
overmarketing. Real efforts should now be made to attack the broader
problems of the Third World, namely, lack of sanitation and education.

569. Salinger, Geoffrey and Richard Sincere.
"The Nestle Tragedy." *The Hoya* September 24, 1982.
The editorial counsels a careful gathering of facts regarding the controversy, many of which it supplies to the reader. The authors stress
the complexity of the issues involved and conclude that Nestle has on
the whole been responsible. This is an example of the campus debate
engendered by the dispute.

570. "Shareholder Resolutions Mushroom in Number Target MNC Operations."
Business International August 13, 1982.
This article refers to the increase in the number of corporate resolutions
introduced at shareholder meetings having to do with an activist
cause. The article describes the failure of INFACT to convince the
SEC to allow it to keep its request for information about sales to
Safeway on the Safeway proxy statement. The SEC ruled that the
proposal was outside the purview of Safeway's activities.

571. Tagliabue, John.
"Pruning Nestle's Operations." *The New York Times* January 3, 1983.
For those tracing the effects of Nestle management changes on the
policy of Nestle in the formula controversy, this item contains information about the "pruning operations" conducted on Nestle operations
by Nestle's Chief Executive Officer, Helmut Maucher.

572. "Truths on Baby Formula."
Bethpage Tribune (New York), p. 4, February 25, 1982.
A representative of Bristol-Myers explains to a local Rotary Club that

there was no substantial data connecting the marketing of infant formula with decline in breastfeeding where declines have been observed. In most countries, there have been no dramatic decreases in breastfeeding.

573. "Union Ends Nestle Boycott."
Healthwire 5(3), March 1983.
The American Federation of Teachers/Federation of Nurses and Health Professionals, by action of its executive council, voted to end that union's boycott of Nestle products. The union had joined the boycott in 1979. The reasons given for the change of position are that Nestle has endorsed and abided by the WHO Code.

574. "Why Are Soviet Babies Dying?"
The Wall Street Journal, February 9, 1983.
Although not dealing directly with the infant formula controversy, this article notes some interesting facts for those contemplating the issues of the controversy. In the Soviet Union, absent market promotion and capitalism, doctors have generally favored the use of powdered milk reconstituted with water. Because such a formula contains little vitamin D, compared with Western formula, babies in the U.S.S.R. have been suffering increasingly from rickets. The Soviets sought help from Abbott Laboratories in building a plant that would produce enriched formula for Soviet babies. It came on line in mid-1980.

575. Wild, William H.
"Infant Formula Swindle Revisited." *Journal Herald* (Dayton, OH), September 17, 1983.
The author concludes from his reading of the Nestle Infant Formula Audit Commission Reports and of Fred D. Miller's booklet on the controversy (See entry number 525) that the accusations against the infant formula companies have been exaggerated.

D. CRITIC GROUPS

576. "Annual Report on Multinational Corporations 1981."
Multinational Monitor 3(1):15, January 1982.
This publication seeks to expose the failings of multinational companies. One part of this issue is devoted to observations by Doug Johnson, director of the Infant Formula Action Coalition. Johnson charges Nestle with trying to defeat the WHO Code, then opposing its adoption by individual countries, and with financing research favorable to its own position. Johnson fits the behavior of Nestle into the larger picture of technological, economic and political control multinationals are said to exercise.

577. Bartimole, Roldo.
"Nestle Pressures Notre Dame Students, Tries Splitting Church Critics." *Multinational Monitor* 9:11, September 1982.
This article says Nestle conducted a campaign on the campus of the University of Notre Dame where a student vote on the Nestle issue

was to be taken. Nestle's nutrition center is labeled an "Orwellian outfit." Furthermore, the author says Nestle called its opponents Communists and cynically hates church opponents while giving the appearance of wanting to cooperate with them.

578. "Confronting the U.S. Infant Formula Giants."
Corporate Examiner July/August 1982.
This issue of the *Corporate Examiner* is devoted to the infant formula controversy with emphasis on the structure of the infant formula industry. The authors cite certain grants and gifts the formula companies have given to pediatric associations as characteristic of the manner in which these companies exercise their influence. Wyeth is described as profit-oriented and American Home Products as being "unmatched" in its "aggressiveness." This issue summarizes beliefs and suspicions of those opposing the infant formula industry.

579. Grant, James P.
"The State of the World's Children, 1982-83." New York: Interfaith Center on Corporate Responsibility, Infant Formula Program, 1983.
This is a report based upon U.N. and other sources, distributed by INFACT, which claims that tens of thousand of babies die each day from malnutrition related to improper formula feeding.

580. Hamilton, Lynn.
"Beyond the Nestle Announcement: What the Critics Say." *The Food Monitor* May/June 1982.
This essay reflects the suspicion that Nestle will not actually comply with the WHO Code even though it agreed to do so.

581. Hogan, Lee Claire.
"Background to a Boycott," *Food Monitor* May/June 1982.
This essay calls for more action against Nestle, listing items people should boycott and addresses to which one may write for more information.

582. Interfaith Center on Corporate Responsibility.
"What Industry Must Do to Conform to the Code." NY: ICCR, undated.
This shortened reprint of the WHO Code has been highlighted and annotated. The activist group's general support for the Code is evident.

583. Interfaith Center on Corporate Responsibility.
"Battling the Bottle: World Health Authorities Condemn Industry Practices." NY: ICCR, c. 1983.
This mimeo contains quotes from delegates at the 36th World Health Assembly in Geneva during May of 1983. Most are condemnations of recent practices of the infant food industry and call for more vigilance on the part of the World Health Organization and governments.

584. Interfaith Center on Corporate Responsibility.
"In Support of the Nestle Boycott." NY: ICCR, Infant Formula Program, February 25, 1983.
ICCR and its infant formula program issued this flier to explain why, at that time, the ICCR still supported the boycott. The flier says that

violations of the WHO Code still exist. There is dissatisfaction with progress made in the controversy. However, the publication gives some evidence that the dispute was "winding down" at this point.

585. Interfaith Center on Corporate Responsibility.
"Milestones: Ten Years of Struggle to Prevent 'Bottle Baby Disease'." NY: ICCR, c. 1983.
This publication presents the highlights of each year for ten years beginning in 1973. The highlights are biased against Nestle, but nevertheless provide a useful chronology.

586. Interfaith Center on Corporate Responsibility.
"Summary Critique of Nestle's October 1982 Policy Statement." NY: ICCR, c. 1983.
This pamphlet expresses the boycotters' continued discontent with Nestle's attempts at self-regulation.

587. International Baby Food Action Network.
"Breaking the Rules: An IBFAN Investigation into the Aggressive Promotion of Artificial Infant Feeding." Minneapolis: IBFAN, May 1982.
This report was compiled by the International Baby Food Action Network (IBFAN) whose participant organizations in various countries have supported the Nestle boycott. Included in IBFAN, for example, are: U.S. INFACT, Interfaith Center on Corporate Responsibility, INFACT, Canada, and the Third World Action Group of Berne. The report lists violations of the WHO Code it alleges occurred. The listings refer to about 30 companies from the very large to the small and local. Much of the promotional material cited may be residual — labels, calendars, and posters not yet out of circulation. Other allegations do not appear to violate the Code in letter or spirit; for example, on page 31: "France (12 Jan. 82) Nestle sponsors seminar/debate on infant feeding for pediatricians, obstetricians, gynecologists, midwives, and GPs." Researchers might want to compare the Nestle Audit Commission Report with this report to determine how many of the alleged violations the Audit Commission agrees are actual violations.

588. International Baby Food Action Network.
"Bringing the Code Home." Minneapolis: IBFAN, 1982.
This publication suggests steps that consumer action groups can take to encourage governments to adopt the WHO Code as part of their national legislation. Steps suggested are the creation of citizen groups, the writing of press releases, the contacting of policy-makers, and the petitioning of members of the infant formula industry.

589. International Baby Food Action Network.
"A Dangerous Trend." Minneapolis: IBFAN, 1982.
This booklet reviews some of the critic groups' most common objections to the promotion of formula feeding in less-developed countries. Mothers have no meaningful choice due to advertising and other promotion forms. Powdered formula is an economic burden for those who can ill-afford to bear it. The article also states that infant formula companies give away free samples and use company sales representatives to promote formula and win over health professionals.

590. International Baby Food Action Network.
"The International Code." Minneapolis: IBFAN, 1982.
This pamphlet explains the adoption of the WHO Code of Breastmilk Substitutes and highlights some Code provisions. Overall, IBFAN is pleased with the Code although they object to ambiguous language regarding the contribution of materials, equipment, and financial help by formula companies.

591. International Baby Food Action Network.
"Loopholes." Minneapolis: IBFAN, 1982.
This pamphlet views the efforts of the International Council of Infant Food Industries (ICIFI) to encourage countries to adopt an ICIFI-proposed code of marketing as an attempt to convince governments to pass into law relatively weak and meaningless code provisions. The writers favor the WHO Code because, they say, it has fewer loopholes and contains an enforcement mechanism.

592. International Baby Food Action Network.
"Successful Strategies to Control Marketing." Minneapolis: IBFAN, 1982.
The regulations governing sales and distribution of infant formula by such countries as India, Sri Lanka, and Lesotho should serve as models for other countries. Codes, bottles-by-prescription, and outright prohibition of commercial sales are mentioned as ways of controlling the marketing of breast milk substitutes.

593. International Baby Food Action Network.
"Taming Transnationals." Minneapolis: IBFAN, 1982.
This booklet is an "action kit" which provides instructions, interviewing techniques and printed questionnaires to be used by the recipient to monitor the marketing practices of infant formula and bottle companies. The pamphlet states that information gathered by these procedures is the basis for pressure and action.

594. Margulies, Leah.
"Ten Points of Clarification on the Nestle Boycott." New York: Interfaith Center on Corporate Responsibility, July 1983.
Late in the controversy some evidence indicated that groups had changed their minds in support of the boycott. This letter is an effort to counter any falling away from the boycott which had occurred or was threatening to occur. The article/letter begins with the statement that the boycott is still on, and covers the issues of Nestle compliance, the Nestle Audit Commission, the changes which some church groups had made on support for the boycott and other matters which had caused confusion on the part of some boycotters.

595. Millar, Ron.
"Nestle Claiming New Reforms." *Multinational Monitor* 11:6, November 1982.
This article reports statements by Edmund Muskie that the Nestle Audit Commission is happy with the responses of Nestle. The issuing of new instructions to Nestle dealers and distributors, however, is still not the same thing as compliance with the WHO Code.

596. Talner, Lauri.
"Special Report: Nestle Boycott May Be Inching Toward Resolution." *News for Investors* (Investor Responsibility Research Center, Inc.,) 9(11):217, December 1982.
The writer observes that the October 1982 Nestle instructions on marketing in compliance with the WHO Code, requested by the Nestle Audit Commission, have prompted some critics of Nestle to say that, if there is adequate proof of observance, the boycott may soon come to an end. Some church groups have already withdrawn their support for the boycott.

E. CHURCH PUBLICATIONS

597. Beck, Roy Howard.
"UM Task Force OKs Nestle Plan, Rejects Boycott." *United Methodist Reporter* September 17, 1982.
In mid-September of 1982, the Task Force on Infant Formula of the United Methodist Church passed and issued a unanimous declaration that the UMC should refrain from participating in the boycott of Nestle products because Nestle had made corrections in their marketing of infant formula in Third World countries. The Task Force was created by the UMC's General Conference in 1980, and the Task Force studied the problems of the dispute for two years.

598. Beck, Roy Howard.
"Nestle: U.M.'s Drove Hard Bargain." *United Methodist Reporter* September 24, 1982.
Associate editor Beck quotes Nestle officials as crediting the United Methodist Church's Infant Formula Task Force with convincing Nestle to support and attempt to implement the WHO Code, and also with helping Nestle to devise the idea of an independent Audit Commission, which became the "Muskie Commission."

599. Beck, Roy Howard.
"Formula Debate Takes a New Turn." *United Methodist Reporter* February 4, 1983.
This article about the United Methodists' stance against the Nestle boycott comes late in the controversy. It explains the continuing conflict between the United Methodist Church and sub-units of the Church. The Church itself took a stand against the boycott while certain sub-units of the Church favored the boycott. The article also recognizes that other local formula companies, sometimes state-owned, have not abided by the Code rules which Nestle is called upon to observe.

600. Beck, Roy Howard.
"'Nestle Boycott' Support Wanes." *United Methodist Reporter* July 1, 1983.
This traces the response of the major denominations to the Nestle controversy. Late in the dispute, and in response to Nestle's reported observance of the basic tenets of the WHO Code, some sub-units of the United Methodist Church withdrew their earlier support for the boy-

116

cott. Regional conferences and actions of resistance or continued support are listed.

601. Burns, Gail.
"Nestle Work on WHO Code Fails to Satisfy Boycott Group." *Catholic New Times* July 11 and 25, 1982.
In this item, the author encourages the continuation of the boycott of Nestle products.

602. "Can Boycotting Be Used As a Christian Method?"
United Methodist Reporter March 5, 1982.
This editorialist suggests that a boycott may be a last resort in Christian social action, and he relates his analysis to the formula feeding controversy.

603. "Fourth Report on the Infant Formula Task Force to the United Methodist General Council on Ministries." April 28, 1983.
This report gives a run-down on Nestle's compliance with the WHO Code, then chronicles the Methodist Church's decision process on ending the boycott supported by several church agencies. It decries the vilification of some people and agencies, recommending that the United Methodists not join the boycott and that those participating cease their actions.

604. Howell, Leon.
"For Nestle's 'Auditors', The Test Is Yet to Come." *Christianity and Crisis* 42:261, September 20, 1982.
This article reports passage of the WHO Code and Nestle support of the Code, church responses to the issue, and the creation of the Muskie Commission. It also contains further church objections to the Nestle position via INFACT. It states that critics claim that Nestle "brought heavy influence" to bear on the drafters of the WHO Code.

605. Howell, Leon.
"Nestle Gets a Passing Grade from Muskie." *Christianity and Crisis* November 15, 1982.
Commenting on the Muskie Commission's first report, this article says that Nestle is cooperative and is attempting to comply with the WHO Code.

606. Jennings, Ray.
"Progress Reported in Nestle Compliance with Formula Code." *The American Baptist* January 1983.
Nestle is reported as making progress in its efforts to comply with the WHO Code, according to this story. The news was received by the leaders of the American Baptist Churches, earlier participants in the Nestle boycott.

607. Johnston, Robert L.
"Silent Emergency." *The Catholic Review* p. A-6, April 22, 1983.
The head of UNICEF states that he believes Nestle management now intends to abide by the WHO Code. He says that U.S. companies are most resistant to the Code and suggests that groups boycotting Nestle shift their attention to other firms.

608. Lovelace, John A.
"UMC 'As A Denomination' Won't Join Nestle Boycott." *United Methodist Reporter* November 5, 1982.
　　The decision of the UMC not to join the boycott came as the result of a two-year study by a special task force named for that purpose.

609. "Methodists Focus on Broader Causes of Infant Mortality." *The Covenant Companion* January 15, 1983.
　　This article warns that danger exists in focusing energy upon one target, Nestle in this case, when the health problems of the world's infants go far beyond the halting of promotional efforts by infant formula companies.

610. "Nestle Boycott A Phony Church Issue."
The Presbyterian Layman 15(1):1, January/February 1982.
　　Nestle has been made into a scapegoat for the boycott groups, according to this discussion of the infant formula controversy. The writer says the price of formula has naturally restricted sales and that infant mortality has not been increasing in the world. The article also says that Nestle is observing the WHO Code.

611. "Nestle Marketing Policies Shift Closer to WHO Code."
Keeping You Posted (Newsletter of the United Church of Christ), 17(9B), November 15, 1982.
　　This report to church members states that The United Church of Christ world hunger action coordinator sees real progress in the recent Nestle announcement that it will voluntarily implement the WHO Code.

612. " 'No Boycott' Stance of Nestle Voted for UM's."
United Methodist Reporter May 6, 1983.
　　The United Methodist Church here calls for the withdrawal of support for the Nestle boycott by United Methodists. The church as a whole did not support the boycott although the questions have been studied by church bodies.

613. Ramming, Corine E.
"The Continuing Infant Formula Debate." *The Lutheran* 21:32, January 19, 1983.
　　This article by a Lutheran layperson calls the efforts to ban infant formula shortsighted and unrealistic. The Lutheran Church of America, says this author, supports the male-dominated WHO bureaucracy by supporting the boycott. The enemy is not Nestle but poverty, disease and ignorance.

614. "Recommendations of the United Methodist Infant Formula Task Force to The General Council on Ministries and the Church," September 11, 1982.
　　These recommendations and supporting analysis would put the United Methodist Church behind the WHO Code but not in support of the Nestle boycott. The analysis explains changes Nestle made in its marketing practices over the past five or six years.

615. "Report of the Joint Nestle Monitoring Committee."
Report of Presbyterian Church in the U.S. and the United Presbyterian Church, U.S.A.; Meeting May 11, 1983 at the Presbyterian Center in Atlanta, GA and May 26, 1983 by telephone conference.
The Joint Presbyterian Nestle Monitoring Committee recommends that the United Presbyterian Church, U.S.A. reaffirm its support for the Nestle boycott because Nestle is said not to be in full compliance with the Code.

616. United Methodist Communications News.
"Infant Formula Task Force." April 5, 1982.
The United Methodist Infant Formula Task Force commends Nestle for announcing guidelines and policies for Nestle distributors to bring Nestle into compliance with the WHO Code regulating the marketing of infant formula. The release notes the resignation of Bishop James Armstrong from the Task Force so that he could serve as president of the National Council of Churches.

617. United Methodist Communications News.
"Nestle." September 13, 1982.
The Infant Formula Task Force of the United Methodist Church recommends, as described by this release, that the Council on Ministries of the Church not join in a boycott of Nestle. The General Council on Ministries had previously set up the Task Force to study issues surrounding formula promotion. Later the Council voted that the boycott not be joined.

618. United Methodist Communications News.
"Nestle." November 1, 1982.
In 1980, the General Conference of the United Methodist Church voted to delegate the authority to support or not to support the Nestle boycott to its General Council on Ministries. After two years of study by a special infant formula task force, the Council voted at this point not to join the boycott. The denomination warns, however, that it will continue to monitor and to expect information from Nestle about progress made in complying with the WHO Code. The release also mentions favorably the action of Nestle in setting up the Nestle Audit Commission.

619. United Methodist Communications News.
"Domestic Hunger." May 9, 1983.
At this conference of Bishops of the United Methodist Church, the Bishops agree to support the decision of the General Council on Ministries not to join the Nestle boycott, and they also agreed to ask annual conferences and agencies which have been participating to continue considering an early end to their participation.

620. "Voluntary Responsiveness to Ethical Concerns by Businesses Welcomed."
The United Methodist Reporter 125(50), May 21, 1982.
This editorial talks about the creation of the Nestle Audit Commission as a sign of business responsiveness to the ethical questions raised by church groups. The writer says that such an independent commission would, in the long run, be a more productive method by which to raise

certain issues of business accountability than adversarial boycotts.

F. INFANT FOOD INDUSTRY PUBLICATIONS

621. Nestle.
"Nestle 1981: The Group's Activities". In: *1981 Annual Reports*. Vevey, Switzerland: Nestle S.A., 1982.

This report contains a wealth of information for the researcher interested in the products manufactured by Nestle and where they are produced. Also included is financial information about the corporation. On pages 10 and 11 of the "Group Financial Results" one finds profits as a percentage of turnover from 1972 through 1981.

622. Nestle.
WHO International Code of Marketing of Breastmilk Substitutes.
"Instructions to All Companies of the Nestle Group and to Agents and Distributors Who Market Infant Formula under Trademarks Owned by the Nestle Group." Vevey, Switzerland: February 1982.

Detailed instructions were issued by Nestle to their dealers and distributors telling them specifically what the provisions of the WHO Code would mean to their business operations. The instructions are organized in such a way that the dealer can read the appropriate WHO Code section and then read the Nestle instructions interpreting and applying that particular provision.

623. Nestle.
"Charter, The Nestle Infant Formula Audit Commission (NIFAC): Washington, D.C.: Nestle Coordination Center for Nutrition, Inc., May 1982.

This document is a copy of the Charter of the Nestle Infant Formula Audit Commission (NIFAC). The function of the Commission as outlined in the charter is to inform the Nestle Company about any problems called to its attention concerning Nestle's failure to comply with the WHO Code or with other similar codes regulating the sale of infant formula. The Commission is to be composed of eight members. Nestle chooses the chairman and has the right to consult with the chairman, church leaders and other groups to determine who shall fill out the membership of the Commission. The Commission is to make quarterly reports and establish its own rules of procedure.

624. Nestle.
WHO International Code of Marketing of Breastmilk Substitutes.
"Instructions to Companies of the Nestle Group and to Agents and Distributors Who Market Infant Formula under Trademarks Owned by the Nestle Group." (Revised). Vevey, Switzerland: October 1982.

After consultation with the Nestle Audit Commission and in response to some experience with the instructions, Nestle issued revised instructions several months after issuing the first set. The revised instructions were substantially the same as the previous ones except that the duty not to promote to the general public was made somewhat stronger by certain changes in wording. Also, a new complaint form created by NIFAC was included. The form was to be used to lodge allegations of violations of the Code with NIFAC.

625. Nestle.
Aide Memoire II. Washington, D.C.: Nestle Coordination Center for Nutrition, Inc., January 29, 1983.
In the second memo to the United Methodist Church Infant Formula Task Force (the first memo was dated September 25, 1981) from Nestle, three steps that Nestle has taken to abide by the WHO Code are described: (1) formation of the Nestle Infant Formula Audit Commission chaired by Edmund S. Muskie to receive allegations of violations of the WHO Code. (This commission is often called the "Muskie Commission"); (2) Nestle's instructions to its distributors and dealers about observing the WHO Code; and (3) Nestle's establishment of a system of worldwide auditing of its own marketing practices.

626. Nestle.
The Nestle Case. Washington, D.C.: Nestle Coordination Center for Nutrition, Inc., April 1983.
This collection of documents and a later revision contain those articles, statements, and other materials which Nestle believes will help one who is trying to understand the Nestle controversy grasp its basic contours. Of course, one would not expect to find the materials of Nestle's opponents in the collection, but Nestle does include many church and audit commission documents which cannot be considered altogether favorable to Nestle.

627. Nestle.
Aide Memoire III. Washington, D.C.: Nestle Coordination Center for Nutrition, Inc., April 28, 1983.
In this, the third memo (the first and second were sent September 15, 1981, and January 29, 1983, respectively) to the United Methodist Church Infant Formula Task Force from Nestle, Nestle narrates its frequent meetings with church and boycott groups intended to end the confrontation. The memo points out that demands made by the boycotting groups have increased in number and stringency as Nestle has complied with initial demands.

628. Nestle.
The Nestle Case. Washington, D.C.: Nestle Coordination Center for Nutrition, Inc., September 1983.
This is the second collection of documents detailing many of the issues of the dispute. The controversy is traced from the U.N. Protein Advisory Group Statement #23 made in 1972 to the Fourth Quarterly Report of the Nestle Audit Commission in mid-1983. In this collection an "INFACT Update" is included among the documents, helping the reader to evaluate how INFACT reports events referred to in other documents. A bibliography is included.

629. Nestle Infant Formula Audit Commission.
First Quarter Report. Washington, D.C.: Nestle Coordination Center for Nutrition, Inc., September 30, 1982.
The report is the first of several reports by the "Muskie Commission."

It explains the origin of the Commission, its make-up, and its primary charge, i.e., to receive complaints and allegations that Nestle's marketing practices are not consistent with its public statements. The report also states that the Audit Commission urged Nestle to make changes in its marketing instructions to its dealers about the implementation of the WHO Code. Those recommended changes were substantially made. At the time of the First Quarterly Report, no specific complaints had been received by the Commission although it sent solicitation letters to over 35 groups active in the controversy.

630. Nestle Infant Formula Audit Commission.
Second Quarterly Report. Washington, D.C.: Nestle Coordination Center for Nutrition, Inc., December 31, 1982.
The Second Quarterly Report notes that during the first six months of the Commission's life, the groups boycotting Nestle were very reluctant to participate in the Commission process. Beginning with the International Boycott Committee and the Interfaith Center on Corporate Responsibility, however, groups began to lodge formal complaints with the Audit Commission. The report states that 78 complaints had been received to that point. The Commission Reports say that the complaints are being processed according to predetermined Commission procedures. Fifty-seven of the complaints had, at the time of the Report, been referred to Nestle for response. The remaining twenty-one were returned to INFACT because they were lacking in documentation, such as the names and addresses of the institutions where violations were said to have occurred.

631. Nestle Infant Formula Audit Commission.
Third Quarterly Report. Washington, D.C.: Nestle Coordination Center for Nutrition, Inc., March 31, 1983.
The Commission Chairman, former Senator Edmund Muskie, reports that the central issues being raised by those groups who filed complaints with the Commission seem to be found in some fifteen of the complaints. The Commission, therefore, has focused its efforts on the fifteen complaints as generally representative of the problems of implementation. The Report characterizes Nestle's response to specific allegations as prompt and serious. The Commission was not, at first, fully aware of how difficult and time-consuming it would be to process the alleged violations. The Report contains a recognition of the multifarious problems of monitoring the marketing practices of dealers and distributors in 140 different countries. Overall, the violations the Commission found have been followed with efforts by Nestle to correct them. Various members of the Commission traveled to Africa and Asia to observe the use of infant formula. The Chairman concludes by saying "Nestle's record is not perfect, but it is honoring its publicly stated commitments".

632. Nestle Infant Formula Audit Commission.
Fourth Quarterly Report. Washington, D.C.: Nestle Coordination Center for Nutrition, Inc., June 30, 1983.
Former Senator Edmund Muskie reviews some of the categories of complaints in this Fourth Quarterly Report. Some complaints resulted from simple violations of the Code by Nestle. Others occurred because

instructions about implementation had not yet reached local distributors or because the instructions had been misunderstood. Other complaints were unfounded, and on still others Nestle and the Commission disagreed on the meaning of a WHO Code provision. Most violations had to do with sampling and promotion to medical personnel although there were direct marketing complaints as well. Twenty-one of the complaints, responses and recommendations are included. The Report also contains an interesting letter report from Commission member Mildred Randall on Nestle formula sales in Mexico. She speaks repeatedly of the problem of competitors who fail to abide by the Code. Also, a summary of the proceedings of the "Conference on Breastfeeding and Infant Nutrition" sponsored by NIFAC (Nestle Infant Formula Audit Commission) June 5-6, 1983, is included.

633. Nestle Infant Formula Audit Commission.
Fifth Quarterly Report. Washington, D.C.: Nestle Coordination Center for Nutrition, Inc., September 30, 1983.
This report, issued by Chairman Edmund S. Muskie, explains the continuing work of the Audit Commission in reviewing and ruling upon complaints brought to it. The writer states that much has been accomplished by the complaint review process, although Nestle has disagreed on certain issues with complainants, WHO, or the Audit Commission. The report highlights issues raised by the process, mostly concerning sampling procedures, labeling, gifts to professionals and lobbying efforts with regard to national codes of marketing. Some unfounded and unsubstantiated complaints have been identified.

634. Nestle Infant Formula Audit Commission.
"Complaint Reports of the Nestle Infant Formula Audit Commission." *Fifth Quarterly Report.* Washington, D.C.: Nestle Coordination Center for Nutrition, Inc., September 30, 1983.
This volume contains an analysis of 64 complaints submitted to the Commission. The format of the volume is to state the complaint, when and where it occurred, Nestle's response, the complainant's reply, if any, the Commission's determination and Nestle's corrective action. The complaints are mostly about samples being made available, and about posters, brochures, materials, and labels not being in compliance with the WHO Code.

635. Nestle Infant Formula Audit Commission.
Sixth Quarterly Report. Washington, D.C.: Nestle Coordination Center for Nutrition, Inc., December 31, 1983.
This report highlights the Commission's changing role in the process of monitoring Nestle's compliance with the WHO Code. The report includes complaints about the company, Nestle's response and corrective action when and where needed, and the Commission's analysis of the complaint. The Commission explains that many of the issues raised in the complaints came at a time when Nestle was redefining and modifying its policies. Although there were some violations, Nestle has primarily done an admirable job in implementing the WHO Code in more than 140 countries. The Commission will now take more active measures to verify Nestle's compliance. These steps will include a series of meetings and surveys in the Third World.

636. Pagan, Rafael D., Jr.
Nestle and Infant Formula — A Decade of Controversy. Nestle Pamphlet.
Washington, D.C.: Nestle Coordination Center for Nutrition, Inc., April 1982.
The president of the Nestle Coordination Center argues the Nestle
case by first tracing the history of the debate over formula versus
breastfeeding. If infant formula were not available, much of the world
would suffer more than they are already suffering from poverty and
malnutrition, says the writer. The article tells how Nestle was singled
out, how hearings were held about the issues, and ends with a question
about how positions taken by the opponents of Nestle came to be so
widely held.

637. Pagan, Rafael D., Jr.
"Carrying the Fight to the Critics of Multinational Capitalism." *Vital Speeches*
July 15, 1982.
Pagan, President of the Nestle Coordination Center for Nutrition,
speaks about the tactics and motives of Nestle during the controversy.
He stresses Nestle's gradual realization that it must find among its
opponents those who were operating in good faith and who trusted
Nestle management, and then seek to discuss the central issues with a
constant eye to practical ways in which these differences could be
resolved. Pagan explains the usefulness of discussions with church
leaders, describing them as satisfying and constructive in most cases.
The speech calls for other multinational firms to recognize they cannot
remain aloof from world opinion and policy bodies but must make
continuous efforts to monitor and influence international organizations as activist opponents of multinationals have done.

638. Pagan, Rafael D., Jr.
"My Turn — Nestle and The Infant Formula Controversy." *Empire* (Juneau,
Alaska) July 28, 1982.
The formation of the Nestle Infant Formula Audit Commission
(NIFAC) is announced. The Commission is a final effort by Nestle to
bring the issues, concerns, and doubts of the controversy before an
independent commission for consideration. Such a commission, says
the writer, is unprecedented. It is a risk for Nestle because the Commission may find that it must criticize Nestle. The company is
vulnerable, but it sees the Commission as the only way to end remaining suspicions among critics.

639. Pagan, Rafael D., Jr.
"Issue Management: The Shaping of an Issues Strategy." Washington, D.C.:
Nestle Coordination Center for Nutrition, Inc., October 25, 1983.
The speaker refers to the public relations aspects of the formula
feeding controversy. He states that international business enterprises
will never be able to defend themselves against the attacks of opponents unless what they are doing is ethical and useful. Pagan then
describes how Nestle diagnosed the objectives of its opponents and
opened dialogue with those groups whose ostensible and inarticulated
objectives were consistent with one another and aimed at promoting
infant health. Pagan also describes the creation of the Nestle Infant
Formula Audit Commission.

640. Pagan, Rafael D., Jr.
"Issue Management: No Set Path." Washington, D.C.: Nestle Coordination Center for Nutrition, Inc., November 7, 1983.

These remarks explain that Nestle, S.A. decided in 1980 to undertake a new effort to deal with its opposition by forming a separate entity staffed by people with expertise in food, science, nutrition, political and sociological disciplines. Pagan also states that changes in policy and the full support of top Nestle management were required in order to overcome the campaign which had sullied Nestle's commercial reputation. The writer contends that business can be profit-oriented while at the same time being decent and ethical.

641. Ross Laboratories.
"Ross Laboratories Pediatric Nutritionals." D495. Columbus, Ohio: Ross Laboratories, June 1982.

This publication shows a new label created by Ross Laboratories which will aid mothers, who speak and read only Spanish or who do not read at all, to correctly prepare concentrated infant formula. Booklets, posters and formula preparation aids are presented.

642. Schwartz, Harry.
"New Campaign Attacks Marketing of Drugs in the Third World." *Commitment* (Abbott Laboratories) Summer 1982.

The writer mentions the infant formula controversy only in passing, but he says that well-organized campaigns are being formed to attack the sale of drugs by pharmaceutical companies into less-developed countries in the same way that infant formula companies had been opposed. He maintains that drug firms have been bringing benefits to underdeveloped countries, where poverty and disease are very serious.

643. Wyeth Laboratories.
"Policy of Wyeth Laboratories and Its Worldwide Affiliates with Regard to World Health Organization International Code of Marketing of Breast-Milk Substitutes." New York: Wyeth Laboratories, (Division of American Home Products Corporation), November 1982.

These are Wyeth company policies with respect to the WHO Code of Marketing of Breastmilk Substitutes, to be observed by all divisions and affiliates. The Code provisions are stated along with Wyeth's comments.

V. THE END OF THE CONTROVERSY: 1984

A. GENERAL ARTICLES AND STUDIES

644. Food Industry Newsletter.
"Industry and the Consumer." *Consumer Update* Fourth Quarter, 1984.
An article in the Harvard Business Review, "Who Cast the First Stone?", by Father Oliver Williams is reviewed here. The review focuses on William's suggestions to corporate managements on how

to handle consumer complaints supported by church-affiliated groups. Williams refers to the Nestle boycott and Gulf & Western's worker relations in its Dominican Republic sugar operations. This issue also comments on a reconciliatory meeting between Nestle executive, Rafael Pagan, and the Christian Church, Disciples of Christ.

645. Greer, Thomas V.
"The Future of the International Code of Marketing of Breastmilk Substitutes: The Socio-Legal Context." *International Marketing Review* p. 33, Spring/Summer 1984.
This article examines the future of the WHO Code while taking no position on the Code's merits. The author says that widespread implementation and adoption will be difficult and will take several years, despite the desire of less-developed countries to regulate international business and to strengthen economic relationships with developed countries.

646. Manoff, Richard K.
"Learning a Lesson from Nestle." *Advertising Age* p. 16, February 13, 1984.
Manoff explains that, after publicity exposed patterns of "indefensible marketing behavior," the major infant formula companies became "captives of their own obduracy." Manoff's thesis is that business theorists will remember the Nestle boycott as a classic case of mis-marketing a good product, ignoring the ensuing problem, and finally, mismanaging the inevitable crisis.

647. Mauk, Susan.
"Breastfeeding and Work." *Working Woman* p. 43, April 1984.
The author discusses the problems that can arise when women working outside the home make the decision to breastfeed their babies. The article contains suggestions on how mothers can keep their jobs and still breastfeed, but states that infant formula is probably a necessity, if only as a back-up to frozen supplies of stored breast milk.

648. Wexler, Celia Viggo.
"The Politics of Breastfeeding." *Empire State Report* p. 33, September 1984.
The author discusses the tensions between groups like INFACT and the U.S. infant formula companies now that the Nestle boycott has ended. Wexler also examines American attitudes toward breastfeeding and how special interest groups have encouraged New York legislators to pass new laws favorable to breastfeeding.

649. Williams, Oliver.
"Who Cast the First Stone?" *Harvard Business Review*, September/October 1984.
This analytical article examines the controversy surrounding Gulf & Western Industries' activities in the Dominican Republic as well as the Nestle boycott. Williams is especially interested in the role church groups played in both struggles. He observes that both corporations and their critics must share the blame for the antagonism existing between the two groups. Williams says that perhaps the corporations are to blame for not responding more publicly and more quickly at the outset, but the critic groups did not work for reconciliation when the

corporations evidenced more responsibility. The author concludes that while some church groups eventually did adopt mediating roles, perhaps they should have done so sooner.

B. SCIENTIFIC ARTICLES AND STUDIES

650. Cashin, Fergus.
"A Formula for Human Kindness." *Doctor* p. 18, February 23, 1984.
The author believes that Nestle's compliance with the boycotters' demands, particularly the concession to acknowledge the superiority of breastfeeding on product labels, may be insignificant compared with other developments. This observation was prompted by an article in the *United Nations Children's Fund Report* for 1984, which claims that an effective treatment has been found for diarrhea — the largest cause of infant mortality in the Third World. The treatment, called "oral rehydration therapy", (ORT) could save millions of infant lives a year. UNICEF says that ORT could halve the present infant mortality rate of 40,000 deaths a day in the Third World by 1990. Cashin recognizes that, while Nestle and other infant formula companies may have contributed to the mortality rate through aggressive marketing practices, mothers cannot be tied to breastfeeding for more than a year, that after five or six months, breastfeeding alone is insufficient, and that infant malnutrition and infection cannot be eliminated without education. In light of this, the author says that it would cause chaos if Nestle were to close down its infant formula operation. Cashin implies that the boycotters may have pushed too far and that recent medical breakthroughs have made the controversy moot.

C. NEWS ARTICLES

651. "Boycott Against Nestle Over Infant Formula to End Next Month."
Wall Street Journal p. 46, January 27, 1984.
This item comments briefly on the anticipated end of the Nestle boycott.

652. "Ethics and Infant Formula."
Boston Globe, February 6, 1984.
The editors conclude that the end of the boycott shows that a protest can be effective, that companies who change their marketing tactics do get credit, and that efforts can be made successfully on behalf of the health of the world's children.

653. Grant, Linda.
"Boycott Ended, Nestle Turns Its Attention to Growth in U.S." *Los Angeles Times,* February 5, 1984.
This analysis recounts the Nestle boycott and then says that Nestle will have to turn all its efforts to maintaining its markets in the United States. These markets have been little affected by the Nestle

boycott. In fact, Nestle sales rose during the boycott. There is no way, however, of knowing just how many sales have been lost as a result of the boycott, say industry spokesmen.

654. Jenks, Susan.
"Nestle Boycott Ends, Firm Revises Tactics." *Washington Times* p. 2A, January 27, 1984.
This story reports the announcement of the end of the Nestle boycott. After nearly seven years of not buying and encouraging others not to buy Nestle products, Doug Johnson of INFACT and Nestle officials broke candy together to celebrate the end of the conflict.

655. Kaufman, Alma.
"Boycott of Infant Formula Makers Expanding." *Cleveland Plain Dealer,* July 15, 1984.
This article notes that the International Nestle Boycott Committee (INBC) and the Infant Formula Action Coalition (INFACT) have begun to put more pressure on U.S. infant formula companies to comply with the WHO Code.

656. Kupferscmid, David.
"Boycott Over Nestle Infant Formula Ends." *Los Angeles Times,* October 5, 1984.
This article notes the termination of the Nestle boycott and mentions that the International Nestle Boycott Committee has said that U.S. manufacturers of infant formula deserve public sanctions because of objectionable marketing techniques in the Third World.

657. Nestle.
"Nestle Boycott Is Over." *Nestle News* p. 1, January 1984.
This account reports the announced suspension of the Nestle boycott by the International Nestle Boycott Committee. It explains how disagreements about the meaning of certain Code provisions were finally clarified.

658. "Nestle Boycotters Say Their Campaign Is Over."
The Boston Globe, January 27, 1984.
This article notes the end of the Nestle boycott campaign. Douglas Johnson, leader of the boycott in the Unitd States, is quoted as saying that "Nestle has moved forward to become a model for the whole industry."

659. Slade, Margot and Wayne Biddle.
"Easing Up on Nestle." *New York Times*, January 29, 1984.
The authors of this report say that persuasive scientific evidence links bottle feeding with disease and death, especially in poor countries. They also say that Nestle has made real changes in their marketing practices.

D. CRITIC GROUPS

660. Clarkson, Fred.
"The Taming of Nestle: A Boycott Success Story." *Multinational Monitor* p. 14, April 1984.
Calling the agreement with Nestle a major victory for the international consumer movement, this article recounts the boycott's history. The author says the end of the boycott may be a help to Nestle, but that it has had a rather disconcerting effect on certain activist groups, such as the International Baby Food Action Network, which have now lost their reason for existence.

661. Happe, Lois.
"People Power Works: A Retrospective of the Nestle Boycott." *Science for the People* p. 10, March/April 1984.
This article reviews the history of the boycott from the viewpoint of a former INFACT leader. The author views the social change effected by the Nestle boycott as only the first step toward even greater changes in larger, more elusive multinational corporations. Most significantly, the boycott effort was a demonstration of the power that ordinary people wield when they organize and cooperate to achieve a common goal.

662. Infant Formula Action Coalition.
"Bottle Baby Campaign — A Decade of Action (Chronology: The Infant Formula Controversy)." *INFACT News* p. 4, Winter 1984.
This illustrated spread depicts INFACT highlights of the boycott from the early 1970s to late 1983.

663. Infant Formula Action Coalition.
"Major Gains in Baby Milk Campaign: INBC Charts What's Left." *INFACT NEWS* p. 1, Winter 1984.
While claiming that "unprecedented gains toward halting inappropriate baby milk marketing" have been achieved, INFACT urges continued support of the boycott until Nestle meets all of INFACT's demands. Many of the demands were met shortly afterwards.

664. Infant Formula Action Coalition.
"Pressure Building on U.S. Formula Companies." *INFACT* p. 1, Winter 1984.
This article notes that, because Nestle is no longer as aggressive as it used to be, INFACT and its affiliates can concentrate more time and energy on pressuring U.S. infant formula companies into full compliance with the WHO Code.

665. Infant Formula Action Coalition.
"INFACT — What We Have Won." Minneapolis: INFACT, January 25, 1984.
This memo from INFACT details the terms of the boycott settlement, including changes made in Nestle's policies and procedures after the four final demands were issued on December 15, 1983.

666. Infant Formula Action Coalition.
"Victory: Together We Won A Victory for Babies." *INFACT Update,* February 1984.
This issue of *INFACT Update* contains articles lauding the resolution

of the boycott as a victory for the boycotters. The success is attributed largely to "several years of grassroots activism" and a "tremendously successful" boycott. One article exhorts people not to forget the value of individual human lives in an economic system driven by impersonal market forces. Nestle, however, is commended for taking the "leadership role" in industry's compliance with the International Code.

667. Infant Formula Action Coalition.
"Victory Of, By, and For the People." *INFACT News*, March 1984.
This issue of the *Update* includes news articles, personal observations, and congratulatory letters claiming a victory for the boycotters. The general thrust of the issue is that consumers can unite and become stronger than large multinational corporations.

668. Infant Formula Action Coalition.
"For the Children, For Ourselves." *INFACT Update*, April 1984.
In these remarks given at the March 1984 Boycott Victory Ball in Boston, Douglas Johnson of INFACT discussed the significance of the agreement with Nestle. First, the agreement translated "moral guidelines" into "practical implementation steps" Nestle would follow. Because Nestle's compliance could be crucial in compelling other infant formula companies to comply with the Code, Johnson said that one million infant lives could be saved every year in the 1980s. Second, Johnson said that the boycott's success "proved that international grassroots organizations can be effective and should continue to be used." Third, Nestle was forced to recognize INFACT and its coalition as legitimate and to deal with it in good faith. In conclusion, Johnson emphasized that the activist movement still had much work to do to ensure that Nestle remains in compliance with the agreement.

669. Infant Formula Action Coalition.
"The Issue Is Global Survival." *INFACT News*, December 1984.
In this issue, INFACT people say they have "expanded" rather than "shifted focus." A victory is declared over Nestle, and a war is declared on nuclear arms.

670. International Baby Food Action Network.
"New Strategies for Baby Foods Campaign." *IBFAN News* p. 1, March 1984.
This article reports the meeting of the second International Baby Milk Conference, co-sponsored by the International Nestle Boycott Committee and the International Baby Food Action Network. While the conference recommended suspension of the six and a half year boycott of Nestle, it emphasized that coordinated international action was still needed to ensure the protection and promotion of breastfeeding and to curb aggressive and inappropriate marketing of commercial baby milk.

E. CHURCH PUBLICATIONS

671. Howell, Leon.
Corporate Power Yields to People Pressure." *Christianity and Crisis* p. 138, April 16, 1984.
Howell views the outcome of the boycott as beneficial to both sides of

the controversy. For the "activists," the resolution was satisfying because it showed that a handful of people in the United States could successfully demand that a major foreign-based corporation make dramatic changes in its sales techniques. Nestle, on the other hand, can now boast of being, perhaps, the corporation most responsive to a changed set of social priorities. Howell praises both sides: the boycotters for having brought worldwide attention to the plight of Third World infants, and Nestle for being a corporate leader "in looking not just at profits but at the social dimensions of its activities."

672. Kane, Matt.
"Anatomy of A Boycott." *Catholic Bulletin,* March 8, 1984.
This is an historical recounting of the Nestle boycott, emphasizing the role of the University of Minnesota's Catholic Newman Center in providing vital support to INFACT during its developing stages.

673. Wall, James M.
"Campbell Boycott Decision Nears." *Christian Century* p. 1027, November 7, 1984.
In an article on the boycott of the Campbell Soup Company, the author discusses briefly the influence of church organizations, such as the National Council of Churches and the World Council of Churches, in negotiating an end to the Nestle boycott. Wall comments that, although initially the boycott harmed Nestle economically and hurt its public image, Nestle is now seen as a model of responsible corporate behavior.

F. INFANT FOOD INDUSTRY PUBLICATIONS

674. "Joint Statement of Nestle and The International Nestle Boycott Committee, January 25, 1984."
Washington, D.C.: Nestle Coordination Center for Nutrition, Inc., January 26, 1984.
This joint statement was signed by Dr. Carl Angst, Executive Vice President of Nestle, S.A., and William P. Thompson, representing the International Nestle Boycott Committee (INBC). It marked INBC's suspension of the boycott of Nestle products. Both Nestle and INBC stated a commitment to the WHO Code and identified four areas related to the Code that required additional efforts in order to bring about an agreement. Nestle agreed to implement the necessary changes in these four areas of concern: educational materials, hazard warning on labels, gifts to health professionals, and free supplies to hospitals. INBC stated that Nestle's progress in these four areas would be evaluated and that, in the fall of 1984, a final decision would be made regarding the termination of the boycott.

675. "Joint Statement of Nestle and The International Nestle Boycott Committee, October 4, 1984."
Washington, D.C.: Nestle Coordination Center for Nutrition, Inc., October 4, 1984.
This joint statement, signed by Dr. Carl Angst, Executive Vice President of Nestle, S.A., and Mrs. Patricia Young, representing the Inter-

national Nestle Boycott Committee (INBC), announces the full termination of the international boycott of Nestle products. INBC acknowledges Nestle's satisfactory implementation of the WHO Code with respect to educational materials, hazard warnings on labels, and gifts to health professionals. The statement also mentions the development of the "Tejada Plan", designed to solve many of the difficult problems surrounding the provision of formula supplies to hospitals. This official statement ending the boycott depicts the two adversaries, Nestle and INBC, as now cooperating in achieving mutual goals.

676. Nestle.
"Nestle Statement of Understanding." Washington, D.C.: Nestle Coordination Center for Nutrition, Inc., January 25, 1984.
The Joint Statement between Nestle and INBC, issued the same day as this document, narrowed differences between the two groups to four issues and marked a temporary suspension of the boycott to give Nestle sufficient time to institute the necessary policy and marketing changes. This Statement of Understanding is Nestle's interpretation of the requirements inherent in the four points and its plan to meet those requirements quickly and efficiently. Regarding the educational materials, Nestle agreed that such material given to mothers will strongly emphasize the benefits and processes of breastfeeding and will sufficiently warn mothers of the dangers of inappropriate formula feeding, as well as its economic costs. Nestle approached the second point, hazard warning on labels, by agreeing to print labels containing effective warnings of the dangers of unclean water, dirty utensils, improper dilution, and faulty storage. Regarding personal gifts to health professionals, Nestle stated that they would severely limit such giving, perhaps even exceeding WHO Code requirements. Regarding the fourth point, supplies, Nestle recognized several definitional ambiguities that would need to be clarified by WHO and UNICEF before full compliance could be achieved. In the meantime, Nestle promised closer enforcement of the proper use of formula supplies to hospitals.

677. Nestle.
"Statement by Rafael D. Pagan, Jr., President, Nestle Coordination Center for Nutrition, Inc." Washington, D.C.: Nestle Coordination Center for Nutrition, Inc., January 26, 1984.
This is a portion of the statement made by the President of the Nestle Coordination Center on January 26, 1984. It does not include his other comments or answers to questions.

678. Nestle.
"Implementation Agenda: WHO Code of Marketing of Breastmilk Substitutes, Nestle Communique Number 1." Washington, D.C.: Nestle Coordination Center for Nutrition, April 25, 1984.
This document publicly sets forth Nestle's efforts to implement the Statement of Understanding that grew out of the Joint Statement of January 25, 1984. This communique announced that Nestle market managers or agents had been notified of present and future refinement of policy in conformance with the WHO Code. The communique also contains a progress report on the implementation of each of the four

points contained in the Statement of Understanding; namely, educational material, hazard warnings on labels, gifts to health professionals, and supplies.

679. Nestle.
"Implementation Agenda: WHO Code of Marketing of Breastmilk Substitutes, Nestle Communique Number 2." Washington, D.C.: Nestle Coordination Center for Nutrition, June 12, 1984.

On January 25, 1984, Nestle and the International Boycott Committee signed a Statement of Understanding stating what the Code required in the following four areas: educational materials, hazard warnings on labels, gifts to health professionals, and supplies. This is the second in a series of communiques intended as public manifestation of Nestle's efforts to implement the Statement. This communique summarizes the progress in the above four areas from April 25 to June 11, 1984. Nestle discusses the testing procedures of the Program for Appropriate Technology in Health to ascertain the most effective formula instructions and hazard warning to be included on labels and in educational material. Nestle also announces that its marketing personnel have been instructed to discontinue all gifts of a personal nature to health professionals and that it issued an Approved List of Inexpensive Materials of Professional Utility That May Be Given to Health Workers. It was further noted that, with respect to the use of supplies, both Nestle and INBC were awaiting further clarification from WHO and UNICEF.

680. Nestle.
"Implementation Agenda: WHO Code of Marketing of Breastmilk Substitutes, Nestle Communique Number 3." Washington, D.C.: Nestle Coordination Center for Nutrition, Inc., July 3, 1984.

This is the third in a series of communiques intended to set forth Nestle's efforts to implement the Statement of Understanding of January 25, 1984, concerning educational materials, hazard warnings on labels, gifts to health professionals, and supplies. This communique focuses on the results of Nestle's combined efforts with an independent firm recommended by WHO and UNICEF to determine appropriate hazard warnings on labels and information to be included in educational materials. The firm working with Nestle, the Program for Appropriate Technology in Health (PATH), conducted several tests to discern reactions to alternative hazard warning statements and formula preparation instructions. The communique contains the specific instructions as well as the proposed hazard warnings that PATH found to be the most effective, and, therefore, recommended Nestle to adopt. Nestle reiterates its intentions to comply fully with the WHO Code and to implement the necessary changes quickly.

681. Nestle.
"Implementation Agenda: WHO Code of Marketing of Breastmilk Substitutes, Nestle Communique Number 4." Washington, D.C.: Nestle Coordination Center for Nutrition, Inc., August 2, 1984.

This is the fourth in a series of communiques concerning educational materials, hazard warnings on labels, gifts to health professionals, and supplies. This particular communique concludes the account of steps Nestle took to complete the revision of their infant formula labels. It also reflects Nestle's commitment to the revision of its educational materials based on field testing and the company's willingness to take the necessary steps regarding its hospital supplies once WHO issues more specific definitions.

682. Nestle.
"Implementation Agenda: WHO Code of Marketing of Breastmilk Substitutes, Nestle Communique Number 5." Washington, D.C.: Nestle Coordination Center for Nutrition, Inc., September 14, 1984.
This is the fifth in a series of communiques, and this particular document summarizes and updates the procedures Nestle has followed to satisfy the first three points covered in the Statement of Understanding: gift policy, development of educational materials, and hazard warnings on labels. Additionally, this communique details the important steps Nestle and the International Nestle Boycott Committee have taken in conjunction with the World Health Organization to bring about the definitions envisaged in the fourth point of the Statement of Understanding dealing with supplies to hospitals.

683. Nestle.
"Addendum to the Nestle Statement of Understanding." Washington, D.C.: Nestle Coordination Center for Nutrition, Inc., September 25, 1984.
This supplement to the January 1984 Statement of Understanding updates Nestle's progress in implementing the four areas specified in the original Statement. Progress was noted in all four areas, but Nestle acknowledged difficulty in the area of supplies to hospitals. Nevertheless, Nestle believes that it is functioning expeditiously within the given time frame and pledges to continue cooperating with WHO, UNICEF, national governments and concerned citizen groups.

684. Nestle Infant Formula Audit Commission.
Seventh Quarterly Report. Washington, D.C.: Nestle Coordination Center for Nutrition, Inc., March 31, 1984.
In this report, the Commission says that, as a result of a series of meetings held in the Philippines, Kenya, and Colombia, it is clear that Nestle has undertaken significant position changes in its marketing practices in the past two years, and according to many meeting participants, Nestle has done far more to conform its policies and practices to the WHO Code than any other infant formula company. NIFAC's main purpose in conducting the meetings was to obtain information on Nestle's current performance in relation to the WHO Code as well as input regarding some of the more controversial and hard-to-interpret provisions of the Code.

685. Nestle Infant Formula Audit Commission.
Eighth Quarterly Report. Washington, D.C.: Nestle Coordination Center for Nutrition, Inc., June 30, 1984.
This Eighth Report contains an analysis of the data obtained as a result of investigations conducted by the Commission in eighteen Third World nations. The investigations were to determine the extent to which Nestle is complying with the WHO Code. NIFAC representatives met with ten to twenty-five health professionals in each country,

asking each individual a standard set of questions so that the responses could be compared and categorized.

686. Pagan, Rafael D.
"Remarks to the Board of World Ministries, United Church of Christ." Washington, D.C.: Nestle Coordination Center for Nutrition, Inc., June 29, 1984.

These statements focus on the importance of maintaining lines of communication and open dialogue between Nestle and church organizations. Pagan credits the churches with being vital to the settlement of the infant formula controversy and urges them to use their influence to see that the WHO Code is adopted by Third World countries and that other infant formula companies be brought to compliance.

AUTHOR INDEX

*(References are to **annotation** numbers, **not** page numbers.)*

Abbott/Ross Laboratories: 134, 135, 136, 471, 472, 473, 474, 475, 476, 477, 478, 479, 480
Aberbach, Pauline: 153
Abrams, Elliott: 154, 155, 208, 357
Addy, D. P.: 058, 232
Adelman, Carol: 156, 512, 539
Adelman, Kenneth: 513
Adeniyi, Adeoye: 137
Administrative Committee on Co-ordination: 157
Ahn, Chung Hae: 158
Aho, Colleen: 358
Adiou, J.: 233
Alakija, W.: 234
Allain, Jean-Pierre: 419
Allen, S. R.: 529
Almroth, E. G.: 235
Almroth, S.: 159
American Academy of Pediatrics: 160
American Home Products Corporation: 478, 479, 480, 481, 482, 483
American Lutheran Chruch: 457
Anderson, Ann: 453
Anderson, Kurt: 359
Andersson, Mari: 514, 540
Anthony, Catherine M.: 161
Anzalone, Charles: 541
Apple, Rima D.: 162
Ashworth, A.: 227, 529
Astrachan, A.: 117
Aykroyd, W. R.: 001, 002, 041

Back, E. H.: 018
Bader, Michael B.: 042
Baer, Edward: 043, 163, 164, 307, 447
Baker, Frances L.: 236
Ball, Robert: 165, 515, 542
Ballabriga, A.: 138
Ballarin, Oswaldo: 332-A
Banks, Pamela: 044
Barness, Lewis A.: 111, 362
Barovick, Richard L.: 363, 516
Barrell, R. A. E.: 237, 238, 313, 314
Barter, I. S.: 484
Bartimole, Roldo: 577
Basford, J.: 087
Bauer, E. Steven: 139
Baum, J. D.: 296
Baumslaug, Naomi: 239
Beatty, Sharon: 166
Beauchamp, Tom L.: 517
Beaver, M. W.: 003

Beck, Joan: 366
Beck, Roy Howard: 454, 597, 598, 599, 600
Behar, M.: 059
Belizan, Jose M.: 333
Bellanti, Joseph A.: 530
Bellini, James: 167
Benderly, B. L.: 112
Berg, Alan: 004, 014, 060
Bickerstaffe, George: 518
Biddle, Wayne: 659
Black, A. E.: 105
Blodgett, Timothy B.: 044
Bolton-Maggs, Paula H.: 240
Borden, Stanley P.: 455
Boyd, John L., III: 259
Bradshaw, Thornton: 169
Bressani, R.: 036
Briesemeister, L. H.: 272
Briscoe, John: 241
Bristol-Myers Company: 478, 479, 480, 485, 486, 487, 488
Brooke, Jim: 368
Brown, E.: 422
Brown, J. E.: 061
Brown, K. H.: 242
Brown, R. C.: 061
Brown, Roy E.: 005, 243
Bruning, Fred: 369
Buchan, Jane: 170
Bullough, Vern L.: 171
Burns, Gail: 601
Burns, Karen: 456
Butler, M.: 277
Butz, William P.: 172, 251
Bwibo, Nimrod O.: 244

Canadian Paediatric Society: 173
Cantrelle, P.: 015
Carhart, Tom: 544
Cashin, Fergus: 650
Center for Science in the Public Interest: 062
Chandra, R. K.: 174, 245
Chase, Anne: 248
Chavez, A.: 024, 063
Chavez, Lydia: 371
Chetley, Andy: 423, 519
Ciocca, Henry G.: 489, 490
Clarkson, Fred: 175, 424, 660
Clawson, Eloise: 202
Clement, Douglas: 425, 426
Coble, R. J.: 536
Cole, Elizabeth: 176
Committee on International Nutrition Programs: 247

Connell, Christopher: 546
Constable, Elinor: 177, 248
Cooke, T. M.: 204
Cottingham, Jane: 045
Cox, David O.: 332-B, 491, 492, 493
Crain, Lance: 178
Cramer-Huerman, J.: 427
Crawford, M. A.: 065
Crow, Rosemary A.: 066
Culbert, Mike: 375
Culley, Phyllis: 249
Cunningham, Alan: 067, 250
deCourcy-Hinds, Michael: 548

Davanzo, J.: 251
David, Peter: 520
Davies, D. P.: 068, 179
Dawson, K. P.: 180
Dayal, R. S.: 252
Debavalya, N.: 291
Dobbing, John: 253, 531
Dobrin, Lyn: 118
Docksai, M. Fisk: 376
Donaldson, Thomas: 521
Donoso, G.: 012
Downing, John: 377
Dugdale, A. E.: 016, 255

Early, Tracy: 458, 459
Eastham, E.: 069
Edozien, J. C.: 070, 256
Edson, Lee: 257
Eide, W. B.: 071
Ellestad-Sayad, Judith: 258
Ellwood, Gracia Fay: 460
Emawis, E.: 012
Epstein, Edwin M.: 181

Fallot, Mary E.: 259
Family Life Foundation: 182
Fikentscher, Wolfgang: 522
Fildes, Valerie: 183
Filer, L. J.: 072
Fisher, Paul A.: 461
Fomon, S. J.: 072, 184, 260, 261
Food and Agricultural Organization of the United Nations: 262
Fookes, G. A.: 529
Foran, D.: 379
Forsum, E.: 263
Frank, A.: 046

Frank, S.: 046
Furer, A.: 140

Garson, Barbara: 119
Gaskin, Ina May: 264
Gbajumo, W. O.: 034
Geddes, John M.: 380
Gelardi, Robert C.: 185
Gephardt, Thomas: 381, 382
Gerlach, L. B.: 186
Gilliam, Dorothy: 383
Gilmore, H.E.: 265
Gladwin, Thomas N.: 187
Goessl, Joan: 384
Goldsmith, Clifford: 188
Gomm, R.: 047
Goodwin, Shirley: 189
Gordon, A. G.: 266
Graham, George C.: 017, 267
Graham, Helen: 276
Grant, James: 385
Grant, James P.: 579
Grant, Linda: 653
Grantham-McGregor, Sally M.: 018
Greer, Thomas V.: 645
Greiner, Ted: 073, 074, 159, 226, 268, 532
Griffiths, M.: 227
Gueri, Miguel: 190, 269, 270
Guest, I.: 386
Gunn, R. A.: 271
Gussler, J. D.: 272
Guthrie, George M.: 387
Gyorgy, Paul: 019

Habicht, J. P.: 075
Hakim, P.: 076, 191
Hall, Barbara: 273
Ham, Tsang Ping: 110
Hamilton, Lynn: 580
Hanafy, M.: 020
Hansen, J. D. L.: 274
Happe, Lois: 661
Harrigan, Anthony: 550
Harrison, Neil: 192
Hartwick, Nanci: 193
Helman, Gerald: 275
Helsing, S. E.: 048, 533
Hempstone, Smith: 389
Hendrickse, R. G.: 006
Herbert, Pearl: 194
Hewson, Barbara: 049

Hickel, James: 195
Hicks, Guy M.: 196
Hide, David: 276
Higgins, Kevin: 523
Hillervik, C.: 100
Hilpert, H.: 138
Hirschman, C.: 277
Ho, Zhi-Chien: 278
Hofvander, Y.: 100, 534
Hogan, Lee Claire: 581
Homer, Daryl R.: 294
Hopkins, H.: 279
Hosken, Fran P.: 428
Howell, Leon: 462, 604, 605, 671
Hoyte, R.: 269
Huffman, S.: 280
Human Lactation Center: 077, 197

Inbaras, S. G.: 322
Infant Formula Action Coalition (INFACT): 120, 429, 430, 431, 662, 663, 664, 665,
    666, 667, 668, 669
Intengan, C. L.: 078, 079
Interfaith Center on Corporate Responsibility (ICCR): 121, 130, 131, 433, 434,
    435, 436, 437, 582, 583, 584, 585, 586
International Baby Food Action Network (IBFAN): 438, 439, 440, 587, 588, 589,
    590, 591, 592, 593, 670
International Council of Infant Food Industries (ICIFI): 141, 142, 143, 144, 494,
    496, 497
Ioannou, Lori: **396**
Isliker, H.: 138

Jackson, John H.: 199
Jackson, Thad M.: 499
Jadhav, H.: 322
Jelliffe, D. B.: 007, 008, 021, 022, 080, 081, 082, 083, 084, 281, 282, 283, 284, 285, 286,
    287, 288
Jelliffe, E. F. P.: 082, 083, 084, 200, 282, 283, 284, 285, 286, 287, 288
Jenks, Susan: 551, 654
Jennings, Ray: 606
Joint Nestle Monitoring Committee: 615
Jones, Carolyn: 276
Johnson, Doug: 122, 441, 442, 443
Johnston, Robert L.: 607
Justsum, Peter: 269, 270

Kanaaneh, Hatim: 023
Kane, Matt: 672
Kardjati, S.: 289
Kaufman, Alma: 655
Kazis, Richard: 444

Keller, H. Anton: 397
Kemberling, Sidney R.: 201
Kent, Mary M.: 290
Kenya, Government of: 098
Kevaney, J.: 085
Khalifa, O. O.: 092
Khan, M. A. R.: 070
Khindaria, Brij: 552
King, Christine: 202
King, F. Savage: 533
Knodel, J.: 291
Korcok, Milan: 292
Kuhn, James W.: 051
Kunt, Aylin: 203
Kupferscmid, David: 656

Laditan, A. A. O.: 086
Lambert, J.: 087, 293
Larsen, Spencer A.: 294
Latham, M. C.: 010, 088, 159, 268, 532
Lauber, Edgar: 295
Laurence, B. M.: 065
Lefever, Ernest: 399, 553
Leridon, H.: 015
Linblad, B. S.: 089
Little, G. Daniel: 463
Lonnderdal, B.: 263
Lovelace, John A.: 608
Lucas, A.: 296
Lusinchi, Victor: 400
Lytle, William P.: 463

MacLean, William C.: 158
Madeley, J.: 554
Maletnlema, T. N.: 524
Manderson, Lenore: 535
Manoff, R. K.: 204, 646
Marchione, T. J.: 205
Mardones-Santander, F.: 297
Margulies, Leah: 090, 124, 125, 126, 132, 163, 164, 332-C, 445, 594
Marshall, E.: 555
Marshall, L. B.: 298
Marshall, M. A. C.: 298
Martinez, C.: 024
Martinez, Gilbert A.: 299, 300
Mata, L. J.: 025, 091, 206
Mathews, T.: 401
Mauk, Susan: 647
Mauron, J.: 145
May, Charles D.: 301
McCall, R. B.: 556

Tagliabue, John: 571
Tainton, Edgar M.: 224
Talner, Lauri: 596
Tarnow-Mordi, W.: 103
Taylor, B.: 104
Terpstra, Vern: 056
Thompson, William P.: 463
Thomson, A. M.: 105, 337
Thomson, Peter: 327
Thornton, J.: 412
Tom, Sally Austin: 443
Tripp, J. H.: 328
Tyrrell, R. Emmett: 413

Ukoli, F.: 234
Underwood, B.: 318
United Methodist Infant Formula Task Force: 603, 614
United States Department of State: 329, 330
United States House Committee on Foreign Affairs: 331, 527
United States Senate Committee on Human Resources: 332
Urrutia, J. J.: 091
Uyanga, J.: 225

Valasquez, Manuel G.: 528
Van Esterik, P.: 226
Villar, Jose: 333
Vitale, Joseph: 236
Viteri, F. E.: 036
Vogel, David: 169

Wade, N.: 107
Walker, A. R. P.: 334
Walker, Betsy: 450
Walker, Isobel: 335
Wall, James M.: 673
Walter, Ingo: 187
Waslien, C. I.: 070
Wasserman, Ursula: 414
Waterlow, J. C.: 227, 336, 337, 338
Watkinson, M.: 339
Webbe, Stephen: 414
Weichert, Carol: 108
Weinstein, Louis: 340
Wexler, Celia Viggo: 648
White, Alison: 270
Whitehead, R. G.: 109, 313, 315, 341, 342, 343, 344, 345
Wickstrom, Bo: 037, 057
Wild, William H.: 417, 575
Willems, G. M.: 427
Williams, Oliver: 649

144

PUBLICATION INDEX
*(References are to **annotation** numbers, **not** page numbers.)*

Academy of Management Review: 320
ACSH News and Views: 221, 537
Acta Paediatrica Scandinavica: 100, 102, 534
Acute Diarrhea: Its Nutritional Consequences in Children: 530
A.D.: 459, 465
Advertising Age: 178, 217, 646
Africa: 554
America: 379, 403
American Academy of Pediatrics: 215
American Baptist: 455, 606
American Journal of Clinical Nutrition: 002, 005, 010, 017, 019, 022, 025, 027, 030, 081, 083, 158, 206, 235, 241, 242, 256, 263, 273, 280, 282, 288, 295, 312
American Journal of Comparative Law: 522
American Journal of Diseases in Childhood: 265, 267, 304, 536
American Journal of Obstetrics and Gynecology: 340
American Teacher: 547
Annals New York Academy of Sciences: 088
Asiaweek: 421
Assignment Children: 218
Archives of Diseases in Children: 018, 068
Arizona Daily Star: 566

Background Paper #38: (FAO): 262
Backgrounder: 196
Baltimore Sun: 565
Barron's: 385, 557
Bethpage Tribune: 572
Boston Globe: 652, 658
Bostonia: 168
Bread and Justice: 207
Breastfeeding and Food Policy in Hungry World: 176, 191, 309
Breast-Feeding in Practice: A Manual for Health Workers: 533
Briefs: 433
Bristol-Myers Annual Report: 486
Bristol-Myers Quarterly Report: 487
British Journal of Nutrition: 086
British Medical Journal: 058, 069, 240, 246, 249, 276, 296, 315, 322, 328, 335
Brooklyn Journal of International Law: 317
Buffalo Evening News: 541
Bulletin of the History of Medicine: 162, 171
Bulletin of the Hong Kong Medical Association: 110
Bulletin of the Pan Am Health Organization: 059, 269, 270
Bulletin of the World Health Organization: 032, 036, 105
Bureau of Public Affairs: 329, 330
Business Abroad: 013
Business Environment/Public Policy: The Field and Its Future: 181, 493
Business and Ethics: 528
Business International: 116, 570
Business and Society Review: 426, 441
Business As Usual: 449

Business Week: 367

New Internationalist: 006, 038, 039, 123, 124, 444
New Republic: 402
New Scientist: 127
New York Journal of Commerce: 396
New York Times: 371, 380, 388, 400, 548, 559, 571, 659
New York Times Magazine: 011, 410
New Zealand Medical Journal: 104, 106, 180
News for Investors: 596
Newsweek: 369, 370, 401
NIFAC Quarterly Repots: 629, 630, 631, 632, 633, 634, 635, 684, 685
Nigerian Medical Journal: 034
Nursing Mirror: 183, 189, 194, 361
Nutrition Bulletin: 253
Nutrition Factor: 004
Nutrition and Human Reproduction: 172, 305, 355
Nutrition: Pre- and Postnatal Development: 287
Nutrition Reports International: 024
Nutrition Research: 245
Nutrition Review: 008, 174
Nutrition Today: 041, 060, 155, 185, 319, 353
N.Y.U. International Law and Politics: 049

Out of the Mouths of Babes: 525

PAG Bulletin: 071, 090, 143
Pakistan Pediatrics Journal: 020
Papua New Guinea Medical Journal: 087
Parents: 556
Peace Corps Times: 166
Pediatrics: 108, 201, 254, 259, 261, 299, 300, 301, 316, 354
Philadelphia Inquirer: 546
Pittsburgh Post-Gazette: 543
Policy Review: 512
Population Studies: 003, 015
Postgraduate Medical Journal: 344
Presbyterian Layman: 610
Press Woman: 514
Proceedings of IXth International Congress of Nutrition: 063, 075
Progressive: 117, 219
Protein Advisory Group: 033, 037
Public Relations Journal: 363, 516

Rand Daily Mail: 562
Reason: 195
Regina Leader Post: 563
Regulation: 513
Research in Corporate Social Performance and Policy: 307

San Francisco Chronicle: 561

Saturday Review of the Sciences: 014
Science: 084, 107, 228, 538, 555
Science Digest: 113
Science News: 374
Science for the People: 450, 661
Scientific American: 404
Sharon Herald: 387
Social Perspectives: 098
Social Science and Medicine: 225
Society: 186
South African Medical Journal: 216, 274, 334
Studies in Family Planning: 163, 226, 286

Tages Anzeiger: 498
Tanzania Food and Nutrition Center Report: 524
Tender Gift: Breast Feeding, The: 053
Third World Institute: 442
Thirteenth Symposium of the Swedish Nutrition Foundation: 089, 091
Time: 114, 359
Toronto Sun: 377
Transactions of the Royal Society of Tropical Medicine & Hygiene: 097, 237, 314, 339
Trial: 376
Tri-Valley Herald: 375
Tropical Doctor: 234
Tropical Georgia Medicine: 289
Tropical Products Institute Report: 009

United Methodist Communications News: 470, 616, 617, 618, 619
United Methodist Reporter: 454, 466, 467, 597, 598, 599, 600, 602, 608, 612, 620
U.N. University Food and Nutrition Bulletin: 157, 278, 297, 318
U.S. News: 412
UVA Daily: 418

Virginia Journal of International Law: 308
Vision: 167
Visitor: 161
Vital Speeches: 637

Wall Street Journal: 364, 365, 391, 397, 399, 405, 539, 553, 574, 651
Washington Post: 357, 368, 383, 413, 568
Washington Star: 389
Washington Times: 544, 551, 654
West Indian Medical Journal: 021, 026, 028, 035, 268
WHO Chronicle: 230
Women's International Network News: 175, 428
Working Woman: 647
World Business Weekly: 416
World Fertility Survey: 290